Aberdeen

EDINBURGH

York

Manchester

Dublin

UEA

Cambridge

Oxford

Bristol

London

Portsmouth

Paris

Madrid

Berkeley

Yale

Mississippi

Minas Gerais

NATACHA LEDWIDGE

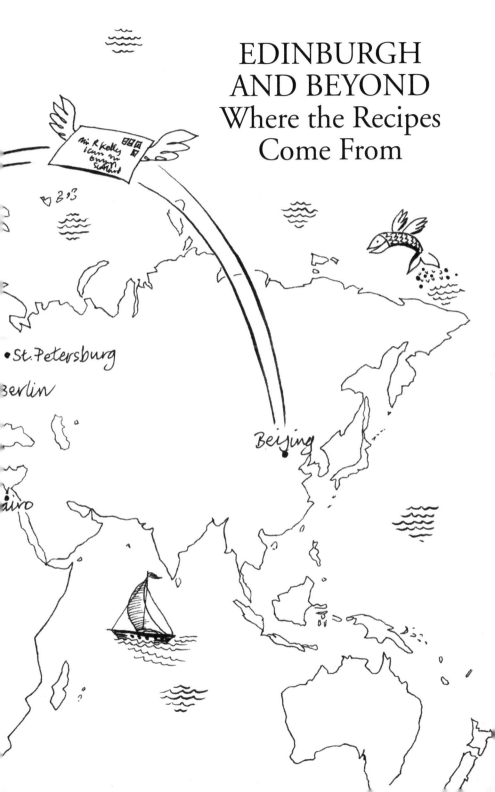

EDINBURGH AND BEYOND
Where the Recipes Come From

Apocryphal student recipe, Leningrad, 1985

GOODBYE

COCKROACH

{PIE}

50 BRILLIANT STUDENT RECIPES FROM EDINBURGH AND BEYOND

Rosanna Kelly and Casilda Grigg

Published by Inky Paws Press

For Sasha, the student cook of the future,
and Caroline and Bobby, friends, always

'The discovery of a new dish does more for human
happiness than the discovery of a new star'

Anthelme Brillat-Savarin, French gastronome

© Rosanna Kelly and Casilda Grigg 2012
Text and illustrations © Individual contributors 2012
Cover illustration by Natacha Ledwidge, back cover illustration by Zebedee Helm
© Individual artists 2012
Published by Inky Paws Press, London 2012
Printed and bound by TJ International Ltd, Cornwall
ISBN 978-0-9574363-0-5
A contribution from the sale of this book will go to Art Refuge UK

NATACHA LEDWIDGE

CONTENTS

ITALIAN PASTAS, RISOTTO & THE ULTIMATE SAUCE

COUSCOUS & CHICKPEAS

EXOTIC ASIAN

BONNY SCOTLAND

ACKNOWLEDGEMENTS

We would like to thank the many friends who helped with this book even though some of them may not remember doing so or we may not have found room for their contributions.

Gail Hallyburton co-compiled the original 1985 cookbook, and Angharad Toms gave invaluable advice from a 2012 student's perspective. Crispin Jackson provided fresh impetus when the cupboard was bare, while Alix Gardner, proprietor of Ireland's longest-established cookery school, showed great patience in answering our questions and setting her students to test our recipes. Derek Westwood for his wonderful design, and Caroline Brooke Johnson for her editorial expertise.

Selma Abbas, Edwina Ashton, Ian Bartlett, Charles Booth-Clibborn, Lulu Bridges, Louisa Burnett-Hall, James Buxton, Susie Casement, Alexandra Chaldecott, Eliza Chisholm, Charles Coleman, Sandra Corona, Jane Dale, Patrick Dillon, Bridget Duxbury, Naia Edwards, Jean Findlay, Simon Foster-Ogg, Thomas Fraser, Rachel Grigg, Sebastian Grigg, Anna Howard, Liane Jones, Henrietta Kelly, Mehreen Kelly, Nicholas Kelly, Christopher Lambton, Stephen Langton, Edmund Limerick, Jo MacSween, Tim Makower, Virginia Marsh, Emma Matovu, Andrew Maud, Simon McGrath, Karen McLachlan, Catherine Milner, Eka Morgan, Patrick Newman, Hetty Neville, Saya Oka, Elizabeth Peyton-Jones, Bonny Ramsay, Jane Richards, Marcus Rees Roberts, Anthony Rockall, Babs Pease, Kate Philipps, Fred Phipps, Sam Phipps, Ivan Samarine, Billie Scarborough, Mary Scott, Caroline Stevenson, Sophie Swire, Isabella Thomas, Inigo Thomas, Danny Tinero, Eric Treuille, Jackie Wan, Elizabeth West, Alex Wilmerding, Greville Worthington.

The illustrators Joanna Chichester-Clark, Justin Hardy, Zebedee Helm, Natacha Ledwidge, Bobby Lloyd, Stella Phipps, Marcus Rees Roberts, Anna Trench.

The student contributors 2012 Becky Arkwright, Angharad Jones Buxton, Ben Cumming, Gabriel Chisholm, Jean-Charles de Boillet, Thomas Kelly, Andrew McKenzie, Mikaël Papantoniou, Rachel Pringle, Sasha Reviakin.

The staff at Brooks Butchers, Kensal Rise.

Our parents Eliane and Anthony, Laurence and Linda.

And last but not least, Anthony Gardner, who has been a guiding force behind this project.

Original artwork from 1985

THE STUDENT COOKBOOK

BOBBY LLOYD

A BOOK TO DIP INTO FOR IDEAS, INSPIRATION AND MERRIMENT

Introduction by Casilda Grigg

WHEN I ARRIVED at Edinburgh in 1986, a nineteen-year-old fresh off the London train, Rosanna Kelly welcomed me, found me a room in a flat above a rackety pub in Cowgate and invited me to arty dinner parties in her beautiful flat on Dundas Street. She was a third-year Art History and Russian student known for her sparkle and flair in the kitchen.

Goodbye Cockroach Pie began life at Rosanna's Edinburgh kitchen table in 1985 after a conversation with Scottish law student Gail Hallyburton in which the pair lamented the lack of cookbooks aimed at students. With the help of Bobby Lloyd, who was studying art at the Ruskin in Oxford, they wrote to hundreds of students in the UK and abroad asking for a favourite recipe (that might be illustrated) to go in a student cookbook. Sadly everyday life quickly took over but years later, chancing on a first draft in a box in her attic, Rosanna was struck by the charm of the illustrations and – with the exception of the cockroach pie from Russia – the engaging quality of the recipes. The result, after vigorous editing and an injection of new talent, is a nod to our Edinburgh days in the mid-to-late Eighties and a compilation of dishes cooked by modern-day students everywhere from Manchester to the Mississippi.

A student thrown into a Tardis and spirited to Edinburgh University in the mid-Eighties would be appalled not just at our fondness for ponchos, Fleetwood Mac and ethnic bags with sequinned elephants, but at our food habits. Yet at the time we loved it all.

Back in the days when Jamie Oliver was a schoolboy and *Crocodile Dundee* was wowing cinema audiences, student meals were built around toast, mince, bacon and breakfast cereals. Potatoes were served baked (a foolproof method) or mashed (nobody knew how to get rid of the lumps). Beans were eaten cold out of the tin and fish only in finger form or wrapped in newspaper. Cheap Chinese was all the rage and nobody drank coffee on the hoof.

(Continued overleaf)

We entertained constantly but we weren't gourmets. Our store cupboards were stuffed with tins and many of our creations were beige in colour. With no Google to resort to, or mobiles to connect us to home, we phoned our mothers for recipes from the payphone in the hall and reached for the Fitou and the Silk Cut when it all went horribly wrong. And yet our meals remain prized and unforgotten. For Laura Pulay (Edinburgh 1986-1989) the height of culinary self-indulgence was two lamb chops with redcurrant jelly in front of *Neighbours*, and for her friend Polly Whately it was tinned macaroni cheese with ketchup on peas.

'CHEAP CHINESE WAS ALL THE RAGE AND NOBODY DRANK COFFEE ON THE HOOF'

The changes of the past 25 years have been dramatic. Where once it was Brie and Roquefort that made our pulses race, students now experiment with all manner of foreign exotica: sweet potatoes, ginger, lemongrass, couscous, chilli. The more ambitious among them make Mexican tacos and Moroccan tagines – dishes none of us had even heard of when we were young.

Yet some of our food habits were oddly prescient. Offal, later championed by London chef Fergus Henderson, was very hot in Edinburgh in the late Eighties. Many a student meal was produced with kidneys or calf's liver and a small charred saucepan. We improvised and were experimental. I remember delicious renditions of haggis with whisky and butter. We supported seasonality and provenance, if only by accident. With no Indian mangoes or Peruvian asparagus to tempt us, we ate an awful lot of home-grown apples, potatoes, onions and carrots.

Now, of course, it's a different story. More choice, more foreign ingredients, a greater variety of fresh food, an even mix of cooking talent among the sexes. Certain dishes remain in vogue – spaghetti Bolognese, carbonara, shepherd's pie, chocolate brownies – but many of today's student cooks make elaborate curries and their own pesto. Some, such as University of London students Angharad Toms and Andrew McKenzie, even grow their own herbs. And many are vegetarian.

Most startling of all, according to Becky Arkwright, who is studying medicine at Edinburgh, they're quite health-conscious. Instead of giving their lungs and liver the standard student pasting, many undergraduates actively load up on fruit and veg in order to hit their five-a-day targets.

The mod cons appear to have improved, if only for a princely few. Rumour has it that Edinburgh students have *dishwashers* in their New Town digs, along with blenders and supersize fridges. But these, says Edinburgh politics student Ben Cumming, are as much a curse as a blessing. 'Dishes are even more likely to pile up, as no one wants to unload the dishwasher.'

Touchingly, many aspects of student life remain unchanged. Breakfast in a greasy spoon is still considered the best hangover cure; Hobnobs – the cantuccini of the 1980s – are apparently making a comeback; and nothing is ever safe in the student *frigidaire*. Novelist and Oxford graduate Anthony Gardner recalls making pancake mix on the eve of a Shrove Tuesday party, only to discover the next morning that his housemates had come home with the midnight munchies. 'They found it in the fridge and just drank it.'

Students will always be students – short of funds, ravenous, adept at improvisation. And this is where *Goodbye Cockroach Pie* comes in. Aimed at young people leaving home for the first time, it is a book to dip into for ideas, inspiration and merriment. Simplicity and speed are the key. Scales are not essential and other than the basics – a fridge, an oven, a ready supply of ingredients – most of the dishes require no more than a sharp knife, a saucepan, a degree of sobriety and a set of friends.

'HOBNOBS – THE CANTUCCINI OF THE 1980S – ARE APPARENTLY MAKING A COMEBACK'

What emerges from talking to undergraduates is that today's student cooking is a distinct improvement on the Eighties. It's tastier, prettier to look at, more cosmopolitan and often better for us. We have gone from malt vinegar and Bulgarian plonk to balsamic and very acceptable Chilean Merlot. We have discovered olive oil, sea salt, fresh herbs, soy sauce. Our taste buds have changed beyond recognition.

How many of us, nostalgic though we might be for the days of Mike Tyson, *Dynasty* shoulder pads and the two-fingered Kit Kat, would really climb aboard that Tardis?

WHAT'S IN THE STORE CUPBOARD?

First-class honours
In the cupboard: the Platonic ideal
Tins of chopped tomatoes, chickpeas, kidney beans, and responsibly sourced tuna; tomato purée; basmati rice; couscous; pasta; lentils; table salt and Maldon sea salt; Dijon mustard; pepper in a pepper mill; red and white wine vinegar; lemons, garlic and extra-virgin olive oil; coconut oil; seeds and nuts; a jar of honey; Parmesan cheese; ginger; cumin, turmeric and other spices; onions; herbal tea.

Diplôme Universitaire
In the visiting French student's fridge
A pot of crème fraîche; 2 pork steaks; fresh mushrooms; vine tomatoes.

2:1
In the cupboard, fridge and freezer
Tea and coffee; some tins of chopped tomatoes and of chickpeas (the basis of quite a few simple meals); lentils; turmeric, nutmeg, oregano; oatcakes; an onion; a bulb of garlic; a lemon; apple cider vinegar; some feta cheese (long-lasting); a full pint of fresh milk; eggs (free-range); unsalted butter; frozen peas.

2:2
In the weekly shopping basket
Lemons; garlic; carrots; potatoes; beetroot; broccoli; tomatoes; a cucumber; a cauliflower; apples; pears; a packet of cheddar cheese; frozen pizza.

3rd
In one Edinburgh student's kitchen
A pot of honey in the fridge; some porridge oats in the cupboard.

Fail
The grim reality
A jar of Branston pickle (nearly empty) and a loaf of sliced white bread (green at one end).

FUDGE IT
ON A BUDGET

How to save every last penny

- Never shop when hungry.

- Nip into your local supermarket between 4pm and 6pm and stock up on freezer-friendly foods with soon-to-expire sell-by-dates (sausages, pork products and fish are regularly discounted). Go any earlier and the reductions will be less; any later, and the bargains may have been snapped up.

- Eat your discounted fish or meat on the day or freeze in individual portions, labelled clearly, wrapped in plastic or sealed in containers.

- Shop at market stalls just before closing time when traders are keen to offload their leftover produce.

- Haggle – sometimes it works.

- Look out for pound-a-bowl discounts. They're a good cheap way to stock up on potatoes, onions, garlic, ginger and lemons – but make sure the produce is still firm to the touch (avocados and tomatoes are often overripe).

- Buy in bulk, especially muesli: scour the aisles for any deals (eg three for the price of two) and split costs with friends/flatmates.

- Save used plastic soup containers for freezing home-made soup, stews etc.

- Slice fresh bread, then freeze and use as required.

- Buy Greek extra-virgin olive oil rather than Italian. It's better value and often just as good.

- Ask your friends for contributions when entertaining. As little as £2 per guest can make a difference if fifteen are coming to dinner. (Always ask at the *beginning* of the evening – after a few glasses of wine you won't remember to.)

- Grow your own mint – it's very easy to do, and high-yielding. Mint and tomato are a very good mix; fresh mint tea is delicious.

JOANNA CHICHESTER-CLARK

THE RED BUS

EDINBURGH FESTIVAL
14-21 AUG 2012
THE
LIST Festival
GREAT TICKET OFFERS

BREAD, PIZZA & SOUP

Sam's Easy Bread

'Making bread is a pleasure – the kneading, the rising, the smell of it baking – and easier than many people think. For a start, there's a huge margin of error with quantities and timings. Once you've made the dough you can turn it into loaves after an hour and a half – or four, five, six hours later. Or stick it in the fridge and forget about it until the next day.

'After a bit of practice you won't even need to measure out the flour and water – you'll know which to add more of and when the texture of the dough is about right.

'Once I read a bread recipe which told me to "knead gently". In fact you can be as rough as you like, grabbing, pummelling, stretching, punching if you must. No harm will come of it – on the contrary, perhaps more air and a better rise.'

YOU WILL NEED:
A large mixing bowl
A wooden spoon
2 non-stick bread tins or a baking sheet
A solid surface to knead on, eg a table
with plastic tablecloth or some kind of
stone or Formica: anything but bare
porous wood, which is hell to clean

INGREDIENTS (MAKES 2 LOAVES)
1kg strong bread flour (wholemeal, white
or any combination)
1 teaspoon of quick yeast
a good pinch of salt
a generous splash of olive oil
2 mugs of warm water
sesame, sunflower, poppy seeds (optional)

- Put the flour, yeast, salt and olive oil and most of the water into the mixing bowl. Stir into a rough, sticky mixture and turn out onto a floured surface. Start kneading with fists, then stretching dough away from you with one palm while clamping the other end down and rolling the whole thing back towards you. Keep at it and in a few minutes you should have a big, smooth, springy ball of dough that is slightly tacky but does not leave much, if anything, on your hands. You may have to add a bit more flour or water and do a bit more kneading to get there.

- Put the ball back in the bowl and work it round the sides until the dough has sucked up any remaining mixture. This is better than washing up the bowl later, when the bits will have set like cement. Cover with cling film and leave. Room temperature is fine, so is cooler or warmer.
- When the dough has risen dramatically an hour or two later, cut it in half and put into the bread tins, pushing down at the sides. An alternative is to shape it in a rough round on an oiled baking sheet. Either way, sprinkle with seeds if you like – patting them into the dough to stop them rolling off – and lastly a dusting of flour. Cover with loose cling film and leave again for about 45 minutes.
- Preheat oven to 220°C/425°F/gas mark 7 and bake on a middle shelf for 45 to 50 minutes. If it's getting very brown on top, turn the loaf upside down for the last 5 or 10 minutes. Overdone is much better than underdone. Cool on a rack (the frames around gas rings often work well if you don't have one) for at least 10 minutes before slicing. By this stage you and your flatmates will be leaping on it. You can also use your own dough for the following two recipes.

Bread Rolls

- Take your risen dough and form half a dozen or so balls in floured hands. No need for a second rise. Place on a greased baking tray with space between them to allow for expansion and bake at 220°C/425°F/gas mark 7 for about 15 minutes. Cool on rack. Eat warm or within a day.

Pizza

Pizza professionals use their hands to conjure the base but a rolling pin is easier.

YOU WILL NEED:
As above, but you will also need:
A baking tray

EXTRA INGREDIENTS
1 jar of passata
1 small packet of cheese (preferably cheddar)
Small quantities of whatever toppings you fancy (salami, mushrooms etc)
A sprinkling of oregano or basil

- When the dough has risen grab a chunk the size of a small apple and roll it out on a floured surface, sprinkling flour on the roller quite often. You want an even base, as thin as possible (only a few millimetres thick).
- Place it on a lightly oiled baking tray of any shape. This does not have to be a special pizza tin. Spread a thin layer of tomato sauce – passata straight from the jar works well – then grated cheese (cheddar is excellent for pizza) and whatever you want in the way of toppings: chopped onions, mushrooms, salami, sweetcorn, capers etc. Be generous, but avoid overloading or the base won't cook properly. Add a little olive oil on top and maybe some oregano or basil plus salt and pepper.
- Put in a preheated oven as hot as you can get it and bake for about 15 minutes or until it looks done. The base should be crisp enough to support a slice in your fingers without total drooping. Scissors are the best way to slice pizza if you don't have a pizza cutter. Eat hot.

Pea and Mint Soup

A sublime pea soup that has the virtue of being cheap yet chic. Serve with a spoonful of crème fraîche and chopped mint on top.

YOU WILL NEED:
A chopping board
A sharp knife
A saucepan
A blender

INGREDIENTS (FOR 6)
a bunch of spring onions
2 sticks of celery
2 cloves of garlic
2 large knobs of butter
3 mugs of water (or vegetable stock)
2 cereal bowls of frozen peas
6 tablespoons of milk
1 vegetable stock cube
4 tablespoons of crème fraîche (1 spoonful for each person's bowl)
fresh mint

- Wash the spring onions, line them up in a row and chop off the roots and any straggly ends. Remove any papery outer leaves. Slice the stems into small circles. Wash and chop the celery. Peel and chop the garlic finely. Melt the butter in a saucepan and cook the vegetables until soft (about 10 minutes).
- Add the water and bring to the boil.
- Add the peas, bring back to the boil and cook until tender (about 3 minutes).
- Remove from heat and allow to cool. Stir in the milk and crumble in the vegetable stock cube before whizzing in a blender. Taste and season with salt and pepper. Pour the soup into separate bowls. Add the crème fraîche and tear a few mint leaves over each bowl.

Egyptian Lentil Soup

According to one Egyptian student, this cheap, tasty and nutritious soup is very good for the complexion. It is also perfect for vegans.

YOU WILL NEED:
A saucepan
A blender or a sieve

INGREDIENTS (FOR 4)
6 cloves of garlic
1 onion
1 small potato
2 tablespoons of olive oil for cooking
1 bay-leaf
a cereal bowl of red split lentils
3 mugs of water
the juice of one lemon and another lemon cut into quarter segments
a few pinches of ground cumin
a few coriander leaves
flat (pitta) bread

- Peel and chop the garlic and onion, and cut the potato into evenly sized cubes.
- Heat the olive oil in a saucepan, then add the garlic, onion, potato and bay-leaf. Cook over a low heat for a few minutes.
- Wash the lentils in cold water two or three times and drain. Stir the drained lentils into the vegetables, pour in the water and cook on a medium flame until the lentils are soft (about 15 to 20 minutes). Add more liquid if they start to dry out.
- Turn the heat off. Remove the bay-leaf and allow the soup to cool. Blend in a liquidiser or mash through a sieve.
- Add the lemon juice and cumin and season with salt and pepper to taste.
- Ladle the soup into bowls. Chop up the coriander leaves and add as a garnish to each bowl. Serve with flat bread and lemon wedges.

Eka's Gazpacho

This zingy tomato-based summer soup is just the thing to see you through exam week. Super-healthy, vegan and packed with vitamins, it can be stored for up to three days in the fridge. Gazpacho can also be served as a main course with side dishes of croutons, chopped hard-boiled eggs (not for vegans), chives and chopped green peppers to dip into.

YOU WILL NEED:
A sharp knife
A chopping board
A blender
A large bowl

INGREDIENTS (FOR 6)
12 medium-sized sweet, ripe tomatoes
2 cloves of garlic
a quarter of an onion
1 cucumber
1 red pepper
1 yellow pepper
1 slice of white bread (crusts removed)
2 tablespoons of red wine vinegar
4 tablespoons of extra-virgin olive oil
cayenne pepper (optional)

- Take a chopping board and a sharp knife and prepare all the vegetables. Chop the tomatoes, peel and chop the garlic, onion and cucumber, deseed and chop the peppers into small chunks.
- Put the vegetables and bread into a blender and liquidise, gradually adding the vinegar, followed by the olive oil.
- Pour into a large bowl and season with salt and pepper to taste.
- Refrigerate for at least 30 minutes.

The soup may be thinned with ice cubes depending on the juiciness of the tomatoes. The flavour should have a bit of zap (owing to the garlic) but shouldn't sting; sprinkle sparingly with cayenne pepper for extra zing. Only serve in summer.

Pão de Queijo (Brazilian Cheese Buns)

These little cheese breads are simple to make, unusual and fun. They're perfect for breakfast and as little snacks. Manioc flour is a gluten-free flour made from the root of the South American cassava plant. Seek out a Brazilian shop and look for a yellow packet saying 'Yoki' on it, and specifying 'Manioc Starch Almidón Dulce'. You can use tapioca flour – stocked by many health food shops and also gluten-free – as a substitute.

YOU WILL NEED:
A large mixing bowl
A saucepan
A wooden spoon
A baking tray

INGREDIENTS (MAKES 20 BUNS)
500g packet of sweet manioc starch or tapioca flour
1 dessert spoon of table salt
1 mug of milk
half a mug of sunflower oil
3 eggs
400g mild ready-grated cheddar cheese (ready-grated will save time)

- Take a large bowl and place the starch or tapioca flour and salt in it.
- In a small saucepan boil the milk with the oil. As soon as it is bubbling over, add to the starch/flour in the bowl and stir in with a wooden spoon.
- Add the eggs and grated cheese and, as soon as it has cooled sufficiently, mash the mixture into a dough with your hands. It will be sticky.
- Cover the bowl with cling film and leave in the fridge for 3 hours. The dough should no longer be sticky. Preheat the oven to 180°C/350°F/gas mark 4. Shape the dough into small buns by rolling the it in the palm of your hand then bake them for 20 minutes. You can also freeze the raw dough buns and cook from frozen.

TASTY THINGS ON TOAST
(and emergency snacks)

Grilled Halloumi with Tomato and Basil

A glamorous variation of cheese on toast that's a doddle to make and perfect for vegetarians. Halloumi is a salty Cypriot cheese that's easily found in supermarkets. Any bread will do, although sourdough is particularly delicious.

YOU WILL NEED:
A sharp knife
A chopping board
A toaster
A grill or a griddle

INGREDIENTS (FOR 2)
4 pieces of sourdough bread, or 6 for big appetites
half a packet of halloumi, finely sliced
a generous handful of cherry tomatoes, sliced
a few leaves of fresh basil
black pepper
olive oil (ideally extra-virgin)

- Lightly toast the bread.
- Lay the halloumi over the toast and place under the grill. Once the halloumi starts to melt and brown at the edges, remove and switch off grill.
- Scatter the tomatoes and basil over the top.
- Season with pepper, drizzle with olive oil and serve immediately.

For an even better, smokier version, cook on a griddle. Place the sliced halloumi on a smoking hot griddle and cook on both sides until striped and sizzling. Meanwhile toast the bread. Lay the halloumi on top of each slice of toast, followed by the sliced tomatoes and basil. Season with pepper and drizzle with olive oil.

Guacamole (The Avocado Dip of the Aztecs)

You can find avocados in supermarkets but they are usually cheaper and riper at specialist Middle Eastern shops. (You can check for ripeness by prodding the thin end – if it gives slightly, the avocado is ready for eating, if it gives too easily it's overripe.)

YOU WILL NEED:
A sharp knife
A chopping board
A large bowl
A potato masher or fork

INGREDIENTS (FOR 4)
5 large ripe avocados
2 cloves of garlic
juice of half a lime
Tabasco sauce

- Take a large chopping board. Cut the avocados in two lengthways with a sharp knife, remove the stones using the sharp point of the knife, cut the two halves into two and peel. Peel the garlic and either crush it or chop it very finely.
- Mash the avocados in a bowl with a potato masher (or a fork), add the garlic and mix in the lime juice. Keep tasting and season with salt and pepper and then add a drop of Tabasco sauce.
- Serve immediately, on toast, with nachos or as a healthy dip with raw carrots or to go with hamburgers (see opposite). Yum!

Zen and the Art of the Perfect Hamburger

No student bookshelf in the early 1980s was complete without a copy of Robert M. Pirsig's *Zen and the Art of Motorcycle Maintenance*. This incredibly simple recipe is a homage to the book's combination of spiritualism and practicality.

The secret of a perfect hamburger is to handle the meat as little as possible.

YOU WILL NEED:
A sharp knife
A chopping board
A spatula
A grill pan

INGREDIENTS (FOR 6)
1kg mincemeat
half a large onion
6 burger buns
1 large tomato (for garnish)
6 lettuce leaves (ditto)

- First divide the meat into six equal portions using a knife, then mould each portion quickly and deftly into a ball with your hands. Next use the spatula to flatten each ball as much as you can (thick hamburgers tend to end up burnt on the outside and raw on the inside).
- Chop the onion finely and use half of it to stud the top of the meat, then sprinkle with salt and pepper. Turn the meat over and do the same to the other side. Place on the grill pan, and cook under a hot grill for a few minutes until the meat and onion on top are singed, squashing occasionally with the spatula to get rid of excess fat. Then turn over and cook on the other side. The meat in the middle should be thoroughly cooked.
- While the burgers are cooking, cut the buns in half and heat them at the bottom of the grill, or in the toaster if you prefer. Place each hamburger on the base of its bun with a lettuce leaf and slice of tomato on top. Add the top of the bun, briefly meditate on the beauty of your creation, and then gobble it up.

Becky's Quick Mozzarella and Pesto Pastry

This simple pastry dish is perfect for quick lunches: it takes less than 5 minutes to prepare and cooks in just 15 minutes. Don't overload the pastry or it will not rise.

YOU WILL NEED:
A large chopping board
A sharp knife
A baking tray
A rolling pin

INGREDIENTS (FOR 2)
half a 375g packet of ready-rolled puff-pastry
1 tablespoon of pesto sauce
1 medium packet (250g) of mozzarella cheese
8 cherry tomatoes
1 teaspoon of dried oregano

- Preheat the oven to the time specified on the pastry packet (usually 200°C/400°F/gas mark 6).
- Drain and slice the mozzarella and cut the tomatoes in half.
- On a sturdy, flat surface roll out half of the puff pastry and place it on a baking tray. Put the other half back into the fridge for another day.
- Spread the pesto on it.
- Place the mozzarella and the tomatoes on top, then sprinkle with dried oregano.
- Put it in the oven and cook for about 15 to 25 minutes.

Bowl-and-Spoon Smoked Mackerel Pâté

YOU WILL NEED:
A bowl
A spoon

INGREDIENTS (FOR 4)
2 smoked mackerel fillets (they usually come in packets of four)
1 tablespoon of cottage cheese
1 tablespoon of Philadelphia cheese
juice of half a lemon, plus extra if needed
ground nutmeg (optional)
cayenne pepper (optional)

- Peel the skin off the mackerel fillets and put the flesh into a large bowl.
- Add the cottage cheese, Philadelphia cheese and lemon juice and mash together with a spoon.
- Grind pepper on top and squeeze more lemon juice in to taste. Delicious with toast. Add a pinch of nutmeg or cayenne pepper to serve.

Patatas Bravas and Chorizo (Fried Potatoes and Sausage in a Spicy Tomato Sauce)

A heart-warming dish for meat lovers with lashings of Iberian flavour.

YOU WILL NEED:
A sharp knife
A large chopping board
A saucepan
2 frying pans
A wooden spoon
A slotted spoon

INGREDIENTS (FOR 4)
FOR THE SPICY TOMATO SAUCE
1 onion, peeled and sliced
2 cloves of garlic, peeled and sliced

1 red chilli, deseeded and sliced
2 tablespoons of olive oil
a pinch of cayenne pepper
a pinch of paprika
a 400g tin of chopped tomatoes

FOR THE POTATOES AND CHORIZO BASE
10 medium-sized new potatoes
1 medium-sized chorizo sausage, evenly sliced into 5mm pieces
flatleaf parsley, chopped

- Put the potatoes on to boil.
- Next start on the spicy sauce. Heat a tablespoon of olive oil in a frying pan and cook the onion, garlic and chilli until the onion is translucent and everything has softened. (Don't let the garlic burn and go bitter.)
- Now add the cayenne pepper, paprika and tomatoes and bring to a simmer. Cook gently for about 20 minutes until it has reduced down.
- By now the potatoes should be cooked so you can drain them and slice them evenly ready for frying.
- Heat a tablespoon of oil in the second frying pan until nice and hot and cook the pieces of chorizo. Add the potatoes and fry everything together. Using a slotted spoon so that you discard the fat, transfer the cooked potatoes and chorizo to a bowl. Spoon over the tomato sauce (it should be hot) and sprinkle with the parsley.

Tomato Bruschetta

A much-loved classic.

YOU WILL NEED:
A sharp knife
A chopping board
A toaster

INGREDIENTS (ENOUGH
FOR 4 BRUSCHETTAS)
1 fresh clove of garlic
a handful of ripe cherry tomatoes
4 slices of ciabatta bread
olive oil
a few basil leaves

- Cut the garlic and the tomatoes in half.
- Toast the bread. Rub one side of the toast with the cut edge of the garlic clove.
- Pile the chopped tomatoes on to the ciabatta. Drizzle olive oil over the tomatoes and season with salt and freshly ground pepper. Place a basil leaf on top and eat immediately.

SELMA'S CHEESE ON TOAST
THE RUSSIAN WAY
(**Leningrad, November** 1985)

Buy a loaf of white bread for 16 kopeks at your local *klebdnaya* bread shop in Leningrad. Go to the *rynok* (open market) and get a kilogram of small tomatoes (some to be eaten at a later date). Go to the local *univermag* (supermarket) and buy a half kilogram of butter, wrapped up in brown paper, and a half kilogram of cheese, handed to you over the counter by a great Russian babushka on receipt of a little chit.

Slice the loaf of bread in half horizontally. Spread on some butter. Put on as many slices of cheese as possible as well as some sliced tomatoes. Add pepper and salt. Put under the grill until everything melts.

NATACHA LEDWIDGE

Snazzy Beans on Toast

This is a cheap and stylish snack that's easy to make and a lovely pea-green colour. It doesn't keep so is best made on the day and kept in the fridge until needed, covered in a light film of olive oil. It goes down a storm with broad-bean-haters – just don't reveal the ingredients. Make sure you season this with plenty of salt and add more lemon for extra zing.

A liquidiser is not essential but will produce a smoother version.

YOU WILL NEED:
A medium-sized saucepan
A liquidiser or masher

INGREDIENTS (FOR 2)
a heaped cereal bowl of frozen broad beans (find them near the frozen peas)
1 clove of garlic
juice of one lemon
olive oil (ideally Greek extra-virgin)
4 slices of sourdough (or any rustic white bread)
about 6 slices of Parmesan or Manchego (a Spanish sheep's milk cheese from the La Mancha region)

- Cook the broad beans in boiling water for 3 or 4 minutes. Drain. Refresh under cold water.
- Peel and finely chop the garlic.
- In a blender, liquidise the beans with the garlic, lemon juice and 4 tablespoons of olive oil. If you don't have a blender, mash the beans and garlic together to make a paste, then put in a bowl and mix in the lemon juice and olive oil. Season with salt and pepper.
- Toast the bread. Spoon the beans over each slice, top with slices of Parmesan or Manchego and drizzle with olive oil. Eat immediately.

Journalist Sam White's kitchen, rue de Grenelle, Paris, 1985

FRENCH CLASSICS

Pommes Dauphinoise (Layers of Potato Cooked in Milk and Garlic)

Don't be intimidated by the French title. This is a simple dish consisting of layers of potato cooked in milk, garlic and sometimes cheese. A great addition to any student repertoire, it goes beautifully with all manner of roast meats. It's not a whole meal, but it's incredibly useful all the same and everybody loves it.

YOU WILL NEED:
A shallow ovenproof dish
A potato peeler or a sharp knife
A chopping board

INGREDIENTS (FOR 6)
1 large clove of garlic
a large knob of butter
6 medium-sized all-rounder potatoes
(eg King Edward or Desirée)
1 mug of milk
half a mug of double cream
1 tablespoon of grated Swiss cheese
(optional)
nutmeg for seasoning

- Preheat the oven to 170°C/325°F/gas mark 3.
- Cut the garlic in half and rub the baking dish with it, pressing hard to crush it. Grease the dish with a generous knob of butter.
- Peel the potatoes and slice them as thinly as you can.
- Arrange the potatoes over the bottom of the dish. Pour over the milk and cream (the liquid should not submerge the potatoes). Scatter over the cheese (if using), and season with salt and pepper and a pinch of nutmeg. Place the baking dish in the oven.
- Bake for an hour to an hour and a half until the potatoes are tender and top is golden.

French Dressing (Vinaigrette)

'It has been a common saying of physicians in England, that a cucumber should be well sliced, and dressed with pepper and vinegar, and then thrown out, as good for nothing' – Boswell: *Journal of a Tour to the Hebrides*

YOU WILL NEED:
A small bowl

INGREDIENTS
1 tablespoon of red or white wine vinegar
half a teaspoon of Dijon mustard
3 tablespoons of extra-virgin olive oil

• Mix the vinegar with the mustard and season with a good pinch of salt and a little pepper. Add the oil slowly and mix with a fork until emulsified. NB Always whisk the oil into the vinegar, not the other way around, to emulsify properly.

JOANNA CHICHESTER-CLARK

Quiche Lorraine (Cheese and Bacon Tart)

High on comfort and packed with flavour, Quiche Lorraine is the perfect dish for a small supper party. Serve warm from the oven with a simple green salad dressed with vinaigrette (see opposite). If you are a vegetarian you can fry an onion and mushrooms instead of the lardons.

YOU WILL NEED:
A sieve
A large mixing bowl
A rolling pin
A clean surface to roll the pastry out on
A flan dish, or a medium-sized frying pan with a metal handle that can go in the oven

INGREDIENTS (FOR 6)
FOR THE PASTRY
a heaped cereal bowl of plain flour
1 egg yolk

100g unsalted butter
1 tablespoon of cold water

FOR THE FILLING
100g lardons (cubes of bacon)
100g of ready-grated Gruyère (usually comes in 200g packs)
4 eggs
5 tablespoons of crème fraîche
5 tablespoons of milk
ground nutmeg (optional)
1 tablespoon of vegetable oil

- Preheat the oven to 190°C/375°F/gas mark 5. Grease the flan dish with a little butter and sprinkle with flour.
- Prepare the pastry: sift the flour and a pinch of salt into the mixing bowl, make a hole in the middle of the flour, add the egg yolk, butter and a tablespoon of water. Crumble with your fingers so that the flour and butter absorb the water. If it is too sticky add more flour, if too dry add more water to make a smooth dough.
- Using plenty of flour to prevent the pastry sticking, roll it out on a flat surface using short movements of the rolling pin. When it has been rolled out sufficiently, place the rolling pin at one end, and roll the pastry around it. Unfold it over the flan dish and tidy up the edges. Prick the bottom with a fork and place in the fridge.
- To make the filling: wash or wipe the bowl you have been using for the pastry, and crack 4 eggs into it. Beat the eggs and add the crème fraîche and the milk. Season with nutmeg and salt and pepper.
- Heat a tablespoon of oil in a pan and fry the lardons.
- Take the pastry out of the fridge and spread the lardons and Gruyère over the base of the tart.
- Pour the egg mixture over the lardons and cheese.
- Put in the oven for 35 to 40 minutes. It is ready when the top is golden.

Porc à la Normande (Pork with Caramelised Apples)

This is a simplified version of a classic French recipe. Normandy is famous for its apples. The great advantage of this dish – in addition to its deliciousness – is that pork is inexpensive compared to other meats and frequently discounted in supermarkets.

YOU WILL NEED:
A sharp knife
A chopping board
A saucepan
A frying pan
A wooden spoon

INGREDIENTS (FOR 4)
4 cooking apples, peeled and chopped
a knob of butter
1 tablespoon of sugar
a pinch of cinnamon
1 tablespoon of vegetable oil
4 pork chops
1 tablespoon of Dijon mustard

- Stew the apples in a saucepan with the butter, sugar and cinnamon. Add a tiny amount of water if the apples are getting too dry.
- Heat a tablespoon of oil in a frying pan, add the pork and the mustard and cook thoroughly. Season with salt and pepper.
- Put the pork chops in a serving bowl and serve with the caramelised apple sauce.

Saumon en Papillote (Baked Salmon in Parchment Paper)

Papillote is a French cooking method in which the food is put into a folded pouch and baked. It's simple and quick but looks cheffy and professional. It's also big on flavour but gentle on the waistline (no fat is used). Serve with couscous, chickpeas, lentils or basmati rice.

YOU WILL NEED:
A sharp knife
A chopping board
A baking tray
Baking parchment (or failing that,
tin foil)

INGREDIENTS (FOR 2)
2 salmon steaks
1 lemon
fresh dill (or basil)
a handful of cherry tomatoes, sliced in half
4 spring onions, finely chopped
a splash of white wine (eg Pinot Grigio)

- Preheat the oven to 200°C/400°F/gas mark 6.
- Place the fish on two sheets of baking parchment on a baking tray (or any ovenproof dish).
- Cut the lemon in half. Set aside two thin slices then squeeze the rest over the salmon.
- Add the two lemon halves, the dill, the cherry tomatoes, the spring onions and the wine. Season with sea salt. Fold and seal the pouch.
- Bake for approximately 15 minutes or until the salmon is just cooked.
- Serve immediately, getting your guest to open his/her own parcel.

Pigeon with Mushrooms on Fried Bread

The taste of pigeon has been described as 'grouse with a touch of buffalo'. This 1985 recipe is a flavoursome dish for a winter's evening. In Ireland, where farmers do not like the pigeons destroying their crop, a pigeon may cost as little as 20p. You can save yourself some work by asking the butcher to prepare the pigeon breasts for you.

YOU WILL NEED:
A very sharp knife
A chopping board
A shallow dish and another dish
or plate to cover it
A large saucepan
A frying pan
A wooden spoon

INGREDIENTS (FOR 4)
2 large red onions
4 pigeons
2 mugs of dry white wine
whole black peppercorns
mushrooms
a good-sized knob of butter
a heaped tablespoon of flour
vegetable oil
1 small loaf of sliced brown of bread
a heaped cereal bowl of button parsley

JOANNA CHICHESTER-CLARK

- Peel and slice one onion finely and place to one side on a plate.
- Cut the breasts from each pigeon, removing the skin and any fat. (Hint: cut from the top of the breast inwards until you hit the bone, and then angle the knife downwards towards the thigh). Prick the breasts, season with salt and pepper and drizzle with oil.
- Take half of the chopped onion and put in a shallow dish. Lay the breasts flat on top and cover with the rest of the onion. Add enough wine to cover them and place another dish or plate on top, weighted to squash them down. Leave to marinate for at least one hour. Turn the breasts once during this period.
- Next make the pigeon stock. Take the pigeon carcasses and place in a large saucepan. Add 4 mugs of water, the second onion (including the skin), a few whole black peppercorns. Chop the mushrooms coarsely and add half of them. Bring to the boil and simmer for 2 hours. Sieve the liquid – there should be 2 mugs of stock. If not, add a little extra water to it.
- Cook the remaining mushrooms in butter. Take off the heat and add the flour. Stir in the stock and add the remaining wine. Place back on the heat and stir until boiling. Cook for this sauce for 5 minutes.
- Cut the bread into small triangles, so that there is one for each pigeon breast, just large enough to hold it. Fry the bread, using very hot oil to prevent it going soggy.
- Fry the marinaded pigeon breasts in butter for just 4 or 5 minutes. Place the breasts on each triangle of fried bread and pour the sauce over it. Garnish with parsley. *Bon appétit!*

Pauper's Pancakes (Crêpes with Mushrooms, Parmesan and Parsley)

This modest-sounding dish is a great student standby that's dashingly French and popular with vegetarians. The pancake mix can be made in advance, and is actually better for a night in the fridge – but take heed of the cautionary tale in the Introduction.

YOU WILL NEED:
A bowl
A wooden spoon
A smallish frying pan
A sharp knife
A spatula
A saucepan

INGREDIENTS (FOR 2)
FOR THE PANCAKES
2 eggs
6 tablespoons of plain flour
a drop of vegetable oil
a mug of milk
a knob of butter or vegetable oil

FOR THE FILLING
1 onion
1 clove of garlic
half a dozen medium sized-field mushrooms
vegetable oil for cooking
fresh parsley, chopped finely
Parmesan cheese to grate over the pancakes at the end

BRIDGET DUXBURY

- Put the eggs, flour and a pinch of salt in a bowl and beat until you have a creamy consistency. Start to add the milk little by little. Continue beating until the mixture has the consistency of single cream.
- Add a drop of oil into the mixture. Beat thoroughly to eliminate all lumps.
- Melt half a teaspoon of butter or vegetable oil in a smallish frying pan and wait until it begins to smoke. Pour a drop of the mixture into the pan; if it crinkles and goes batter-like, you can start cooking the pancakes.
- Wait until each pancake is cooked and then turn over with a spatula. When nicely browned, put onto a plate and start the next pancake. You can keep the pancakes warm in the oven until you feel like serving them – but cover them in tin foil so they don't dry out.
- Next set to work on the filling by peeling and finely chopping the onion and garlic, and chopping the mushrooms.
- Heat a little oil in the saucepan at a low to moderate heat and add the onions and garlic. Cook on a very low heat until they are translucent. Then add the mushrooms.
- After 10 more minutes of cooking, place a spoonful of filling into the middle of each pancake and fold over. Sprinkle the grated Parmesan and chopped parsley over the top and serve immediately.

Gabriel's All-in-One Roast Chicken

It's worth splashing out on organic chicken for this recipe. Not only is it more ethical but the flavour is infinitely superior. Whole birds tend to be punitively expensive but supermarket packs of organic thighs and drumsticks are generally better value and occasionally discounted. This is a stylish all-in-one dinner party dish that's virtually stress-free. For a gutsier, less polite version add two chorizo sausages (cut into chunky pieces) halfway through the cooking.

YOU WILL NEED:
A sharp knife
A chopping board
A roasting tin or casserole dish

INGREDIENTS (FOR 4)
several fresh sprigs of rosemary
8 organic chicken thighs and drumsticks
16 cherry tomatoes
16 new potatoes, cut in half
6 shallots, cut in half (shallots are milder and sweeter than ordinary onions)
4 large cloves of garlic (no need to peel or chop)
1 lemon, quartered
1 tablespoon of olive oil

- Preheat the oven to 200°C/400°F/gas mark 6.
- Strip the leaves off the rosemary stems, then chop the leaves in a tight pile.
- Arrange all the ingredients attractively in a roasting tin and cook for at least 45 minutes until thoroughly cooked.

Bœuf Bourguignon (Slow Cooked Beef and Red Wine Stew)

The ideal dinner party dish, this can be cooked in a large saucepan on top of the stove, and is even better made a day ahead. Serve it with rice, baked potatoes or tagliatelle with a green salad to accompany it.

YOU WILL NEED:
A large heavy-based saucepan
A casserole to go in the oven

INGREDIENTS (FOR 6)
1.2kg lean stewing beef in cubes
3 tablespoons of vegetable oil
2 onions
2 garlic cloves

3 generous handfuls of button mushrooms
100g lardons (cubed bacon)
2 tablespoons of butter and an equal amount of flour
half a bottle or more of any red wine (Côtes du Rhône works well)
2 bay leaves
3 sprigs of fresh thyme or half a tablespoon of dried thyme

- Turn the oven on at a low heat 180°C/350°F/gas mark 4.
- Heat the vegetable oil in the saucepan over a high heat until very hot. Season the beef with salt and pepper and add to the saucepan. Let the meat brown nicely.
- Meanwhile peel and slice the onions, chop the garlic and slice the mushrooms finely. Blanch the lardons in boiling water for 1 minute to get rid of the saltiness.
- When the meat is nicely browned, remove from the saucepan and place in the casserole.
- Lower the heat and add the lardons and chopped onions to the juices from the meat in the saucepan. Cook for a few minutes, making sure nothing sticks to the bottom. Next add the butter and flour and mix in. Then add the wine and a little water. Boil for one minute.
- Pour the saucepan contents over the meat in the casserole and add the mushrooms, garlic, bay leaves and plenty of thyme. Season again with salt and pepper.
- Place a lid on top of the casserole and cook the stew slowly in the oven for approximately two hours until the meat is tender.
- Before serving, taste for seasoning and take out the bay leaves and sprigs of thyme.

WHORES' PASTA

ITALIAN PASTAS, RISOTTO & THE ULTIMATE SAUCE

Pasta Puttanesca (Whores' Pasta)

Pasta Puttanesca was daringly ahead of its time in 1985. Now it's positively trendy. Make sure you have a bottle of olive oil at the ready.

YOU WILL NEED:
A sharp knife
A chopping board
A wooden spoon
A frying pan
A large saucepan

INGREDIENTS (FOR 2)
1 tablespoon of olive oil
2 cloves of garlic, peeled and finely chopped
1 red chilli, deseeded and sliced finely or half a teaspoon of chilli flakes
4 anchovy fillets
a 400g tin of chopped tomatoes
a heaped teaspoon of dried oregano
several leaves of fresh basil if available
half a 500g packet of spaghetti
6 caper berries or a tablespoon of capers
6 pitted black olives, halved

- Heat a tablespoon of olive oil in the frying pan over a gentle heat and cook the garlic, chilli and anchovies for a few minutes.
- Add the tomatoes, dried oregano and basil and allow the sauce to simmer for approximately 20 minutes.
- While the sauce is simmering, cook the spaghetti in boiling salted water.
- At the last minute stir the capers and olives into the sauce. Drain the spaghetti. Mix in the sauce and serve immediately.

Angharad's Creamy Courgette Tagliatelle

This quick, easy and delicious pasta sauce is rather luxurious and just the ticket for vegetarians. The preparation won't take more than 10 minutes and the cooking about 15 minutes. Serve piping hot in warmed bowls.

YOU WILL NEED:
A sharp knife
A chopping board
A grater
A large saucepan
A wooden spoon
A large frying pan

INGREDIENTS (FOR 4)
4 large courgettes
4 cloves of garlic, crushed or finely chopped
12-16 nests of tagliatelle
1 or 2 tablespoons of olive oil
half a small glass of dry white wine (Pinot Grigio is perfect)
1 tablespoon of single cream
a quarter of a teaspoon of Dijon mustard
a sprinkle of nutmeg (optional)
Parmesan cheese (optional)

- Grate the courgettes and prepare the garlic.
- Place the tagliatelle in a large saucepan of salted boiling water and simmer gently according to the packet instructions.
- While the pasta is cooking, heat the oil gently in a large frying pan, add the grated courgettes, and after a minute or so the garlic. Cook until soft and slightly golden.
- Add the wine to the courgettes and turn up to a high heat until there are no longer alcoholic fumes coming off the pan. This should take a minute or so.
- Remove the frying pan with the courgettes from the heat and stir in the cream, a little at a time. Stir in the mustard and the nutmeg and season with salt and pepper to taste.
- Check the progress of the pasta. Once it has cooked, drain it lightly and toss it into the sauce. If the frying pan is too small, return the pasta to the saucepan and add the sauce. Serve with grated Parmesan if you like.

Steve's Mum's Spaghetti Bolognese

This much-loved dish is an absolute classic and worth cooking again and again until you can almost do it in your sleep. A lifesaver in 1985, it's never gone out of fashion.

YOU WILL NEED:
A sharp knife
A chopping board
A large frying pan
A wooden spoon
A large saucepan

INGREDIENTS (FOR 4)
1 tablespoon of olive oil
1 onion, peeled and finely sliced

1 clove of garlic, peeled and chopped or crushed
500g beef mincemeat
a 400g tin of chopped tomatoes
2 tablespoons of tomato purée
dried oregano
a whole packet of spaghetti
fresh Parmesan cheese to grate over the spaghetti at the end
a small bunch of flatleaf parsley, chopped

- Heat a little oil in the frying pan, add the onion and the garlic and cook for 1 minute. Add the mince, turning with a wooden spoon until it is cooked through.
- Stir in the tomatoes and tomato purée. Season with salt and pepper and add a pinch of oregano. Simmer on a low heat for 10 minutes. If it gets dry, add a spoonful of water.
- While the sauce is cooking, heat a large saucepan of water (adding a pinch of salt) until it is boiling rapidly. Add the spaghetti, and a small amount of oil to prevent it from sticking; stir. Cover the pan until the water reboils, then take the lid off and turn the heat down slightly. Boil uncovered for the time it says on the packet (usually 10 to 12 minutes) or until just tender. Drain it over the sink.
- Place the spaghetti on warm plates and spoon over the Bolognese sauce. Scatter with the grated Parmesan and some chopped parsley.

Pasta with Fresh Pesto

Making pesto doesn't take long and it is much more delicious than bought pesto in a jar. If you have a liquidiser, place all the ingredients inside and blend to a smooth purée.

YOU WILL NEED:
A large sharp knife
A chopping board
A large saucepan
A large bowl

INGREDIENTS (FOR 2)
half a 500g packet of pasta
2 cloves of garlic
1 large pot of basil
50g (half a regular packet) of pine nuts
one third of a mug of
extra-virgin olive oil
a substantial chunk (about 60g)
of Parmesan

- Put some water on to boil in a large saucepan (it should be about two-thirds full), adding a pinch of salt. When the water is boiling rapidly, put the pasta in, with a small amount of olive oil to prevent it from sticking; stir. Bring the water back to the boil and cook the pasta until *al dente* (soft but with a bite to it).
- While the pasta is cooking, get a large chopping board out. Peel and chop the garlic very finely. Remove the basil leaves from their stems and pile on top of the chopped garlic. Put the pine nuts on top and chop everything again. Put the mix into a large bowl and grate the Parmesan cheese on top. Add the oil. Mix. Now the pesto is ready to put on the pasta.
- Drain the pasta over the sink and tip into a large bowl. Stir in the pesto. Top with more grated Parmesan. Hey pesto!

Pearl Barley Risotto with Butternut Squash

This is a homely, sweet and nutty-flavoured vegetarian risotto. Set aside a good 20 to 25 minutes in order to attend to the stirring. You can peel the squash if you like.

YOU WILL NEED:
A sharp knife
A stable work surface on which to chop
up the butternut squash
A baking tray
A saucepan
A wooden spoon
A grater

INGREDIENTS (FOR 4)
half a butternut squash
2 tablespoons of olive oil
1 onion
2 cloves of garlic
3 handfuls of mushrooms
a cereal bowl of pearl barley
2 mugs of hot vegetable stock (or failing that, water)
1 teaspoon of dried thyme
1 teaspoon of dried parsley
fresh Parmesan or Grana Padano cheese to taste, grated
fresh chopped parsley to garnish

- Heat the oven to 200°C/400°F/gas mark 6.
- Cut off both ends of the squash and then cut the rest of the butternut in half at the waist. Stabilise the half you are using on a sturdy surface. Slice vertically and then cut into cubes. Put the cubed butternut squash onto a baking tray and coat evenly with oil. Season well with salt and pepper and put into oven.
- Peel and dice the onion, peel and finely slice the garlic, and slice the mushrooms.
- Heat a tablespoon of oil on a medium-low heat in a large saucepan and cook the onion and mushrooms until soft (around 5 minutes). Add the garlic, taking care not to burn it.
- Add the pearl barley to the pan, stirring it around for about a minute until it begins to shine. Add the thyme and parsley and season with salt and pepper. Pour in a small amount of hot stock and keep stirring until it has been absorbed. Repeat until all the stock has been absorbed.
- At the last moment, remove the butternut squash from the oven and stir it into the risotto. If the pearl barley is still crunchy, add water in the same way as the stock. Like the pasta on the opposite page, it should be soft, but with a bite – almost *al dente*.
- Stir in the grated cheese and decorate with chopped parsley.

Alix's Tomato Sauce

This is a quick and easy sauce to go with any pasta.

YOU WILL NEED:
A sharp knife
A chopping board
A large frying pan
A wooden spoon

INGREDIENTS
1 onion
1 tablespoon of olive oil
1 clove of garlic
a 400g tin of chopped tomatoes
2 tablespoons of tomato purée
fresh basil

- Peel and chop the onion. Fry slowly in the oil until translucent.
- Chop or crush the garlic. Add to the onion and cook for just 1 minute.
- Stir in the tomatoes and tomato purée. Simmer for 10 minutes.
  Taste and season with salt and pepper.
- Add fresh basil.

GUARANTEED THE CHEAPEST RECIPE ON THE CAMPUS
(And possibly the simplest, in 1985 or ever.)

Cooking time 7 to 15 minutes.

INGREDIENTS
14 pasta shells per person
1 small bad onion (buy on Thursdays
for super cheapness)
A tiny bit of butter
1 tin of cheap Spanish tinned tomatoes
A hint of garlic
a twist of black pepper
a thumb and finger of salt

DE LUXE VERSION ONLY
a little tomato purée

- Cook the pasta shells.
- Chop the onion thinly. Fry in butter till soft. Add garlic, plus the twist, thumb and finger. Stir. Add tomatoes and purée. Stir.
- Serve on a paper plate.

NATACHA LEDWIDGE

Salsa Verde

This vivid green sauce is a great way of adding va-va-voom to chicken, pork, lamb, white fish and vegetables of any kind. Covered in a film of olive oil (with a Keep Out sticker attached), the sauce keeps for a couple of days in the fridge. If you don't have a food processor or blender, chop everything finely by hand – the result will be coarser, but just as tasty.

YOU WILL NEED:
A blender

INGREDIENTS
a small supermarket bag of flatleaf parsley
a small supermarket bag of basil
1 teaspoon of capers, drained and rinsed
2 cloves of garlic, peeled
1 tablespoon of red wine vinegar
half a mug of extra-virgin olive oil (preferably Greek)

• Place all the ingredients in a food processor and purée until smooth. Season (preferably with Maldon sea salt) to taste.

COUSCOUS & CHICKPEAS

Miss R Kelly
1 Grove Terrace
Edinburgh
SCOTLAND
U.K.

Ivan's Couscous for 200

This 1985 recipe is only for mathematicians or very ambitious party-givers!
If there are just 8 of you, you will need just one kettle and one large bowl,
and one cucumber to one 500g packet of couscous.

YOU WILL NEED:
A vast number of bowls

INGREDIENTS (FOR 200)
30kg couscous
enough boiling water to cover the
couscous
enough mint and parsley to fill a
herbaceous border
lots of lemon juice
60 cucumbers, peeled and chopped
extra-virgin olive oil

- Put the couscous into large shallow bowls.
- Just cover with boiling water.
- Cover with lids or plates and set aside for a few minutes.
- Finely chop the mint and parsley. Peel and chop the cucumbers.
- Take the plates off the couscous, add the mint, parsley and cucumbers to the couscous, and dress with olive oil, lemon juice and salt and pepper to taste.
- Fluff the couscous with a fork (or pitchfork).

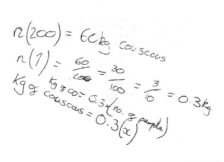

$$n(200) = 60kg \text{ couscous}$$
$$n(1) = \frac{60}{100} = \frac{30}{100} = \frac{3}{10} = 0.3kg$$
$$kg \text{ of couscous} = 0.3 \times (no. \text{ of people})$$
$$kg \text{ of couscous} = 0.3(x)$$

Andrew's Herb-Laden Chickpea Curry

This inexpensive, satisfying and vegan-friendly dish requires minimal washing-up.

YOU WILL NEED:
A sharp knife
A chopping board
A grater
A large saucepan
A wooden spoon

INGREDIENTS (FOR 4 TO 6)
2 tablespoons of vegetable oil
1 onion, finely chopped
3 cloves of garlic, peeled and finely chopped
a 2.5cm chunk of ginger, peeled and finely grated (or 1 teaspoon of ginger powder)
1 heaped tablespoon of medium curry powder
2 large potatoes, peeled and evenly chopped into 1½ inch cubes
2 mugs of vegetable stock
1 teaspoon of dried coriander
1 teaspoon of dried parsley
1 teaspoon of dried thyme
a 400g tin of chickpeas, drained and rinsed
fresh coriander, chopped
rice (optional)

- Heat the oil in a large saucepan on a medium heat. Cook the onion, garlic and ginger until soft (around 5 minutes). Make a thin paste from the curry powder using a little water and add to the onion. Cook until the liquid has mostly evaporated.
- Add the potatoes to the pan and mix until they are coated with the curried onion mixture. Turn up the heat and pour over the stock, ensuring the potatoes are covered. Add the dried herbs. Cook for 20 minutes, stirring occasionally.
- Next add the chickpeas. Cook for a further five to ten minutes. Season to taste with salt and pepper. Sprinkle with the coriander and serve with rice if you fancy.

A Mild Chickpea Curry with Fresh Coriander

This is a subtle curry, but it could be made more ferocious by upping the spices. The basic ingredients – a tin of tomatoes and chickpeas – are inexpensive and can be kept in the cupboard for emergencies, as can long-lasting spices. Pretty to look at and healthy, this can be served as a main meal with basmati rice, or as an accompaniment to other dishes.

YOU WILL NEED:
A sharp knife
A chopping board
A large, heavy-based saucepan
A wooden spoon

INGREDIENTS (FOR 4)
1 onion, peeled and finely chopped
1 clove garlic, peeled and chopped
2 teaspoons of chopped fresh ginger

1 tablespoon of vegetable oil for cooking
1 teaspoon of turmeric
2 teaspoons of medium curry powder
a little chilli powder
a 400g tin of chopped tomatoes
juice of half a lemon
a 400g tin of chickpeas, drained and rinsed
a bunch of coriander and of fresh mint, chopped

- Heat a tablespoon of oil and add the onion and garlic. Cook until soft, then add the ginger and cook for another minute or so.
- Add the turmeric, curry powder and chilli powder, then stir in the tomatoes and lemon juice.
- Add the chickpeas and simmer for 10 minutes. Season with sea salt.
- Sprinkle with the fresh herbs just before serving.

Chickpea and Mint Salad

This makes an attractive and very tasty salad. Serve it unaccompanied as a vegan option or with lamb chops for a more substantial supper.

YOU WILL NEED:
A sharp knife
A chopping board
A salad bowl

INGREDIENTS (FOR 4)
400g tin of chickpeas, drained and rinsed

a generous handful of cherry tomatoes, halved
plenty of mint, torn into strips
1 red onion, peeled and finely chopped
olive oil (Greek, ideally)
a generous splash of lemon juice

- Mix the chickpeas, tomatoes, mint and red onion, then drizzle with oil plus lemon juice. Season with sea salt.

EXOTIC ASIAN

Japanese Meatballs and a Teriyaki Marinade

This recipe is inspired by Harumi Kurihara, who has been described as Japan's answer to Delia Smith. It works well with pork or beef. Use any leftover teriyaki for spooning over grilled salmon or chicken. Mirin is a Japanese rice wine that's sold in oriental shops and larger supermarkets.

YOU WILL NEED:
A small saucepan
A chopping board
A sharp knife
A small bowl
A large bowl
A frying pan

INGREDIENTS (FOR 4)
FOR THE TERIYAKI MARINADE
two and a half tablespoons of soy sauce
two and a half tablespoons of mirin

4 tablespoons of caster sugar

FOR THE MEATBALLS
half an onion
1 stick of celery
1 egg
500g pork mince (or beef mince)
2 tablespoons of plain flour
6 basil leaves
1 lemon
vegetable oil

- Begin by making the teriyaki marinade. Measure the soy sauce, mirin and sugar into a small saucepan. Slowly bring to the boil and leave to simmer on a very gentle heat for about 20 minutes until it has thickened.
- Meanwhile, finely chop up the onion and the celery.
- Take a large bowl and crack an egg into it. Add the onion, celery, mince and flour and combine well.
- Tear the basil leaves into small pieces and add to the mixture.
- Shape the mixture into small meatballs and lay out on the chopping board.
- Heat a little oil until sizzling hot in a non-stick frying pan, then add the meatballs and cook until nicely brown on each side. (You may have to do this in two batches depending on the size of your frying pan.) Keep the cooked meatballs warm in the oven if necessary.
- Pour the teriyaki sauce into a small serving bowl. Chop the lemon into 4 wedges and arrange on the side of a serving plate. Put the meatballs on the plate and serve with the teriyaki sauce. Each person may squeeze a little lemon juice on the meatballs for even greater deliciousness.

Pad Thai (Rice Noodles with Tofu)

The tofu gives the noodles a more subtle flavour than the usual chicken or prawn. Get all the chopping and preparation done before the cooking, which has to be very quick.

YOU WILL NEED:
A sharp knife
A large chopping board
7 cereal bowls
A saucepan
A wok (or a large, deep frying pan)
A wooden spoon

INGREDIENTS (FOR 2)
2 cloves of garlic
a 2.5cm piece of ginger
4 spring onions
2 eggs

150g tofu (often sold in 396g packets)
3 limes
2 tablespoons of unsalted peanuts
1 red chilli, deseeded and chopped
a handful of fresh coriander
1 tablespoon of fish sauce
1 tablespoon of caster sugar
a handful of bean sprouts
sesame oil
soy sauce
2 nests of rice noodles
2 tablespoons of a light vegetable oil, eg sunflower or groundnut oil

- Take the chopping board and the knife and peel and finely chop the garlic and ginger. Place in bowl one. Thinly slice the spring onions and place in bowl two. Crack the eggs into bowl three and beat them. Chop the tofu into small, even cubes and set aside in bowl four. Squeeze the juice of two limes into bowl five. Chop the peanuts and put in bowl six. Deseed and finely chop the red chilli and set aside in bowl seven. Chop the coriander and set aside (to garnish the dish at the end). Cut the third lime into quarters.
- Put the bottle of fish sauce in readiness by the stove, along with the caster sugar, bean sprouts, sesame oil and soy sauce.
- Cook the noodles in a saucepan (follow the packet instructions) and drain.
- Take the wok and heat over a high heat until it begins to smoke. Add the vegetable oil and swirl it around until it is hot, then add the garlic, ginger, and half of the spring onions. Stir-fry until the onions start to soften. Add the egg and stir until it is cooked. Then add the tofu.
- Stir in the rice noodles, mixing in with the egg.
- Next add the fish sauce, chilli, caster sugar, lime juice, bean sprouts and half of the peanuts. Stir-fry for about 30 seconds. Splash over some sesame oil and soy sauce.
- Season with salt and pepper to taste. Serve immediately, topped with the remaining spring onions, peanuts and the coriander. Squeeze juice from the lime wedges to taste

Easy Saag Paneer (Spinach with Indian Cheese)

Don't be put off by the long ingredients list – this is really quick if you are organised with the preparation (about 15 minutes to prepare and 15 minutes to cook). It's packed with flavour and is a great option for vegetarians. Serve with rice, chapatti and/or poppadoms.

YOU WILL NEED:
A sharp knife
A chopping board
A grater
2 large bowls
A large deep frying pan or a saucepan
A sieve
A wooden spoon

INGREDIENTS (FOR 4)
FOR THE SPINACH BASE
250g fresh young spinach (usually sold in 260g packets)
vegetable oil
250g paneer cheese, diced into even cubes (you can buy this ready-cubed in 500g packets)

1 medium onion, peeled and chopped
a small handful of fresh mint, chopped
juice of half a lemon
2 mugs of vegetable stock from a cube
a small handful of fresh coriander, roughly chopped
1 or 2 tablespoons of single cream

FOR THE SPICE MIX
4 tablespoons of olive oil
1 tablespoon of garam masala
1 or 2 fresh red chillies (otherwise use 1 or 2 teaspoons of dried chilli flakes)
4 cloves of garlic, crushed
a 2.5cm chunk of ginger, grated finely
1 teaspoon of ground cumin
1 teaspoon of ground coriander

- Wash and finely chop the spinach. Place in a bowl and pour boiling water from a kettle over it to make it wilt. Drain through a sieve into a bowl, saving the water to use as stock.
- In a saucepan heat a little vegetable oil and fry the paneer cubes until lightly golden. Take the cubes out of the pan and set aside on a plate.
- In a bowl, mix together all the spice-mix ingredients.
- Heat the spice and oil mixture in a large deep frying pan or a large saucepan, add the chopped onion and cook for around 5 minutes until the onion has become soft and translucent.
- Add the spinach to the pan along with the cubes of paneer, mint and lemon juice and simmer gently for 10 minutes, adding spinach water as necessary.
- Remove from the heat, stir in the coriander and single cream. Season with salt and pepper to taste.

Spinach and Sweet Potato Dahl

For curry-lovers with a ready supply of spices, this is a deeply satisfying vegetarian recipe that is relatively cheap and can be frozen in servings. The preparation takes about 15 minutes and cooking time is about 40 minutes. It can be served with rice and/or chapattis; it's also delicious with a raita of plain yoghurt, lemon juice and finely diced red onion.

YOU WILL NEED:
A sharp knife
A chopping board
A grater
A large saucepan with a lid
A wooden spoon

INGREDIENTS (FOR 4 TO 6)
FOR THE SPICE MIX
4 tablespoons of olive oil
4 cloves of garlic, peeled and crushed
a 2.5cm chunk of ginger, peeled and finely grated
1 tablespoon of garam masala
1 teaspoon of ground cumin
1 teaspoon of ground coriander
1 teaspoon of turmeric
half a teaspoon of asafoetida

1 or 2 fresh hot red chillies, deseeded and finely chopped (otherwise use 1 or 2 teaspoons of dried chilli flakes)

FOR THE REST
1 medium onion, roughly chopped
three quarters of a mug of red lentils
3 medium-sized ripe tomatoes, roughly chopped (or a 400g can of chopped tomatoes)
three and a half mugs of vegetable stock (made from a cube) or water
2 medium-sized sweet potatoes, peeled and evenly diced to in approximately 1cm cubes
a cereal bowl of fresh spinach
a small bunch of fresh coriander, roughly chopped

- Prepare the spice mix and heat it in the saucepan over a low heat.
- Add the onion and fry for around 5 minutes, or until soft and translucent.
- Add the lentils to the pan and fry for around 1 minute. Add the tomatoes, the stock and the sweet potato, season with salt and gently simmer for 20 minutes with the lid on, then remove the lid and cook for another 10 minutes, stirring frequently.
- Remove from the heat and stir through the fresh spinach until it wilts. Add the fresh coriander and season to taste.

Kate's Coronation Chicken

People of all generations love this dish. It's easy and quick – and is ideal for large numbers and picnics. Looks aren't its strong point. Adding white grapes and chopped parsley will greatly improve its appearance. If you've got any left-over chicken or turkey, the sauce is a clever way of jazzing them up.

YOU WILL NEED:
A sharp knife
A chopping board
A large bowl
A wooden spoon

INGREDIENTS (FOR 5 TO 6)
1 cooked chicken. (If you buy an uncooked one – poach for 1 hour – put in a large saucepan cover with water, add chopped carrots, celery, onion, peppercorns, bay-leaf, salt and simmer gently; the chicken is cooked when the juice runs clear and joints are loose; the stock can then be used for soups.)

FOR THE SAUCE
a 200g jar of Hellmann's mayonnaise
340g natural yoghurt (three quarters of a large tub)
2 teaspoons curry powder
juice of half a lemon
2 to 3 tablespoons of cream
1 or 2 fresh red chillies (otherwise use 1 or 2 teaspoons of dried chilli flakes)
4 cloves of garlic, crushed
a 2.5cm chunk of ginger, grated finely
1 teaspoon of ground cumin
1 teaspoon of ground coriander

- Cut the meat from the chicken.
- In a serving dish, mix the sauce ingredients – taste and alter proportions as necessary.
- Add the chicken pieces and mix them in thoroughly.

STELLA PHIPPS

BONNY SCOTLAND

Macbeth-style Chicken Cu[rry]

This is a rich aromatic curry with [blocked]. The recipe has been given by
Christopher Lambton, who was a[n en]gineering student at Edinburgh in the
early 1980s. His delicious stews w[ere l]egendary. Now he owns Laurel Bank, a
Scottish tea room that has expand[ed t]o become a bistro and pub for the village
of Broughton in the Borders.

'I first discovered curry when som[e E]dinburgh friends introduced me to the
searing heat of Khushis in Broug[hton] Street – the first Indian restaurant
to open in Edinburgh, in 1947. I [soon] started cooking my own: elaborate
concoctions with spices that wer[e dry]-roasted, ground and added to sauces
with pinpoint precision. This ch[icke]n curry is much less fiddly. It is simple,
quick, and very tasty. It has bee[n desc]ribed as "Macbeth-style" cooking
presumably because the techniq[ue is] little more than chucking everything into
a bubbling cauldron.'

chillies, garlic, ginger, cumin and coriander

YOU WILL NEED:
A sharp knife
A chopping board
An electric coffee grinder (or a p[estle]
and mortar)
A casserole or heavy-based saucepan
A wooden spoon

INGREDIENTS (FOR 4, *if*
accompanied by rice, naan, and
chutney)
2 tablespoons of sunflower oil
1 large onion, finely chopped
several large cloves of garlic, peeled and
finely chopped

1 dessert spoon of cumin seeds
1 dessert spoon of fennel seeds
2 dessert spoons of coriander seeds
1 teaspoon of fenugreek seeds
1 teaspoon of black peppercorns
1 teaspoon of ground ginger
1 teaspoon of ground turmeric
half a teaspoon of ground chilli
4 skinless chicken breast fillets, chopped
into 2cm cubes
half a tube of tomato purée
enough stock or water to easily cover
the chicken
fresh coriander, finely chopped

(Continued overleaf)

- Soften the onion and garlic gently in enough oil so that you can stir them around easily.
- Leave to cook while you use an electric coffee grinder or a pestle and mortar to grind up the whole spices to a fine powder – you may need to do it in two batches. Add this to the powdered spices (be careful not to overdo the chilli – you can always add more later) and mix together well before adding to the onion.
- Stir well over a steady heat until the spices and onion darken: it doesn't matter if they burn a bit. Add the chicken. Stir, allowing the chicken to get coated in the spices and maybe char a little.
- Add the tomato purée and continue to stir. Depending on the moisture in your chicken and onion you now need to add enough liquid to allow the mixture to bubble away in a thick sauce.
- Season: a good curry needs plentiful salt, whatever your doctor might advise. Salt will bring it to life.
- You will need to stir constantly or put the pan into a slow oven and forget about it for a while. It is ready when the chicken pieces are cooked through and firm to the touch: normally about 10 minutes on the stove top but longer in the oven (about 30 minutes).
- Garnish with lots of fresh coriander stirred in at the last minute. Leave to cool and eat the next day for the best flavour.

A Note on Spices

'I am no expert spice mixer. The recipe above only recently acquired ground black peppercorns when I discovered that in small quantities they add an intense, sweet heat distinct from chilli. However, too much black pepper can be overwhelming and very unpleasant, so watch out. Cumin and fennel are similar seeds with an anis background note, so one can be omitted. Fenugreek adds feisty bitterness, but it is probably inessential. Turmeric is mainly for colour. I sometimes add cardamom pods as I love to crunch them open and chew the seeds (great for a sore throat). The only spices that are crucial are chilli and salt. You can effectively waste a whole mess of lovely spice mix if you don't add sufficient heat and seasoning: be bold!

'I grind my spices using a Krups coffee grinder (you can get one for about £20) which has served me well for 30 years, not to mention bringing exciting noise and smells into the kitchen.'

Cranachan (A Crunchy Oat Cream Pudding)

Raspberries folded into double cream and sprinkled with toasted oats and a splash of whisky – what's not to love? This traditional Scottish pudding takes next to no time to make and is good enough for a dinner party. Serve it in wine glasses for a touch of glamour.

YOU WILL NEED:
A grill
A whisk (preferably electric)
2 wine glasses

INGREDIENTS (FOR 2)
2 tablespoons of porridge oats
2 tablespoons of brown sugar
a small pot of double cream
2 tablespoons of fresh raspberries (or from a tin)
a dash of whisky

- Begin by toasting the oats and the sugar under a moderate grill. Turn the mixture continuously to prevent burning.
- Whip the cream until thick and spoon into two wine glasses.
- Add the raspberries and whisky.
- Smother with the toasted oats and sugar.

A Delicious Way of Making Porridge

And healthy too.

YOU WILL NEED:
A saucepan
A wooden spoon

INGREDIENTS (FOR 1)
half a cup of porridge oats
one and a half cups of cold water
a handful of nuts and raisins
a banana

- Put the water in the saucepan, add the porridge oats and stir. Bring it to the boil stirring occasionally, add the nuts and raisins, then reduce the temperature so that the porridge is barely simmering. Cook for about 4 minutes.
- Slice a banana on top, add a sprinkle of brown sugar and a drop of milk or cream if you like.

Haggis, Neeps and Tatties

Haggis is the ultimate student food – it is easy to prepare, economical, satisfying and cosy (in the words of Robert Burns's *To a Haggis*, 'a glorious sight,/Warm-reekin', rich!'). It takes 10 to 15 minutes to prepare and about 45 minutes to cook.

This recipe has been given by Jo Macsween, director of Scotland's leading haggis company. 'Sharing haggis during my student days and beyond has helped to cement many life-long friendships. The most memorable was when I spent a term in Venice and invited my neighbours round for a haggis supper. It was a huge success and my rather modest hospitality was rewarded with countless reciprocal invitations.

YOU WILL NEED:
Tin foil
A casserole dish
2 saucepans
A sharp knife
A chopping board
A masher

INGREDIENTS (FOR 2)
454g Macsween traditional or
vegetarian haggis
2 small neeps (turnips or swedes)
1 carrot to add colour to the neep
3 medium-sized tatties (potatoes) – use a
good mashing variety like Maris Piper
plenty of butter

- Pre-heat the oven to 180°C/350°F/gas mark 4.
- Prepare the haggis for cooking – remove the outer vacuum-pack bag and wrap the haggis in foil. Place in a casserole dish with a few centimetres of water to keep the atmosphere in the oven moist. Cook for approximately 45 minutes. (You can also cook the haggis in a pan of simmering water. Try to keep the water on a gentle simmer – you almost want to 'poach' the haggis. Whatever you do, don't boil it! Do be very careful when lifting the haggis out of the hot water at the end of the cooking.)
- Meanwhile, prepare the vegetables by peeling both the potatoes and neeps. Dice the neeps into 1cm cubes and cut the potatoes in half if large. Peel and chop the carrot. Try and cut the vegetables into equal sizes so they cook evenly. Place the prepared potatoes in a pan of cold, salted water. You will need a separate pan of cold, salted water for cooking the neeps and carrot.
- Bring both pans of vegetables to the boil, and then reduce to a simmer and cook until they are soft (about 20 to 25 minutes). The timings will depend on the size of the chopped vegetables. Test the vegetables with a sharp knife before draining – especially the neeps, as they need to be nice and soft in order to mash properly.

(Continued overleaf)

ZEBEDEE HELM

A Turnip for the Books

- Once the vegetables are cooked, drain them separately and allow all the steam and moisture to evaporate. This will ensure creamy potatoes and neeps that are not watery!
- To mash the potatoes, add some butter, salt and pepper to taste, and get mashing! How much of these ingredients to use is, to a large degree a matter of personal taste, so add a little at a time until you have creamy, lump-free mashed potatoes.
- To mash the neeps, add some butter, and salt and pepper to taste. Neeps are really tasty with butter and black pepper, so don't stint on these! Give the neeps and carrots a good mash, but don't mash until creamy – you want to retain a bit more texture, creating a good contrast to the smoother, creamier texture of the potatoes in the finished result.
- Keep the mashed vegetables warm. Take the cooked haggis out of the oven and check it is hot. The skin should be tight and too hot to touch.
- Hot plates are a must. Cut open the haggis and spoon onto the hot plates, along with the mashed neeps and tatties. Garnish the top with chopped parsley if you wish. (Haggis is also delicious with cooked beetroot, which could be used as a garnish.)

For those who like a sauce with their haggis, you might like to try cream and whisky, cream and mustard, beer and onion, or even mushroom. Whisky is the other traditional accompaniment, but lots of other drinks go just as well, if not better: my vote is for a fairly robust beer. Whether you pour whisky over your haggis is entirely up to you; I would recommend you enjoy them separately.

Express method

If you are time-pressed, there are some short cuts you could take, such as microwaving the haggis. (This amount of haggis would take under 5 minutes – just remember to remove the casing first and chop into chunks.) There are plenty of ready-made mashed vegetables for sale these days, and they take 3 to 4 minutes per pack. The standard pack size is 400g and this would be plenty for 2 people. If you add a sprinkling of parsley and a bit of cracked black pepper on the top before serving, your guests might well believe you did all the peeling yourself.

A Bhompston Trout

Although Bhompston is actually in Dorset, this 1985 recipe by Charles Booth-Clibborn has found its way into this section as a tribute to the Edinburgh-based fishing enthusiasts who hurry off after the week's lectures to pull on their waders and brave a Scottish river.

YOU WILL NEED:
A fishing rod
A very sharp knife
A chopping board
A baking tin
Tin foil

INGREDIENTS (FOR 1)
1 trout (preferably weighing between
350g and 1.35kg)
a few sprigs of fresh rosemary or fennel
fronds
2 teaspoons of butter

- First *catch your trout*.
- Gut it (leaving the head on) under running water. Stick knife into its bottom hole and slice up to the jaw; put finger in, grip, rip, and tear until clean and fishmonger-looking. If you are going to keep the trout overnight, it is better to remove the gills, which can be ripped or cut out – since they are slightly acidic, they can spoil the flavour.
- Alternatively, go out and buy one, ready-gutted. A fresh fish has bright clear eyes and healthy red gills; it shines, and if you press the flesh it shouldn't leave a dent. Fish fillets should also look firm and shiny.
- Lay your trout in a greased baking tin of an appropriate size. Sprinkle the outside and the inside of the trout with salt and pepper.

(Continued overleaf)

JOANNA CHICHESTER-CLARK

- Next insert small amounts of fennel or rosemary into the stomach. Also put a teaspoon of butter inside and outside the fish. If you suspect the fish is muddy, or if the flesh is very white (the better-tasting trout will have orange pink flesh, having fed off freshwater crustaceans), salt the stomach overnight and be more generous with the chosen herbs.
- Cover the trout with baking foil and put in a hot oven (190ºC/375ºF/gas mark 5). A 450g fish should cook for approximately 25 minutes. The flesh should be solid but moist, and should peel off the carcass easily without taking any small bones with it. Do not forget the trout's cheeks – extremely tasty.

An Old-Fashioned Baked Potato with Sour Cream and Fresh Chives

A 1980s stalwart that's delicious when the potato is crunchy on the outside and crumbly inside.

INGREDIENTS (FOR 1)
1 large floury potato (Maris Piper or
King Edward), scrubbed clean
a spoonful of sour cream
a spoonful of chopped chives

- Preheat the oven to quite hot (200ºC/400ºF/ gas mark 6).
- Sprinkle sea salt over the scrubbed potato and then pierce the potato skin with a fork in several places to prevent the potato from bursting in the oven. Put the potato on the middle rack in the oven and bake for about an hour.
- In a smallish bowl mix the sour cream and chives together and season with salt and pepper.
- Once the potato has cooked take it out of the oven, put it on a plate, cut it in half and fill with the mixture. Eat straight away.

Greville's Beef and Apricot Pacific Glory

This landmark 1985 recipe was an early British version of what we now know as a tagine. Modern interpretations replace the steak with lamb and use spices such as cinnamon, cumin, turmeric and paprika.

'The first time I cooked this I had a restaurant cook to dinner who was so taken by it she included it in the menu at McIntoshes restaurant, Stafford Street, Edinburgh, so I know it is a success and both looks and tastes like a Hawaiian sunset. I cooked it in a slow cooker during the day; if you don't have one, then just use a casserole dish and fend for yourself, or you could borrow mine I suppose.'

INGREDIENTS (FOR 4)
1 packet of dried apricots
1½lbs casserole steak (cubed)
2 to 3 fresh young onions

1 cube beef stock
2 to 3 fresh young carrots
1 bay-leaf
1 tablespoon of flour

'Pre-soak the apricots for 3 hours (no more) making sure not to break the skins. Chop the onions and soften in a little oil, making sure they don't go brown. Add the beef slowly and with a great deal of care to ensure it does not turn to rubber. Place in a slow cooker with the stock and the chopped carrots and bay-leaf. Cook the stew for as long as possible to allow the meat to become tender. Add the apricots and leave to simmer on auto setting until they are ready. Serve with baked potatoes with a little butter and lots of black pepper. Make sure everyone has enough apricots.

'Only serve this recipe in the winter months as the idea is to fill up with good and nourishing food while at the same time enticing the palette with the apricots to evoke the splendours of a summer tropical paradise.'

NATACHA LEDWIDGE

BOBBY LLOYD

PUDDINGS, CAKES & ICES

A Quick Chocolate Mousse

This divine chocolate mousse requires minimal shopping and can be made a day ahead. Make sure the melted chocolate has had enough time to cool down before you add it to the yolks.

YOU WILL NEED:
Two large bowls
A hand or an electric whisk
A saucepan

INGREDIENTS (FOR 6)
170g (just under two standard-sized bars) dark chocolate (Lindt 70% is a good one)
several tablespoons of sugar
6 eggs
a large pot of double cream (optional)

- Melt the chocolate very gently with the sugar and leave to cool.
- Separate the eggs, setting aside the whites and beating the yolks.
- Gradually add the melted chocolate mixture to the yolks. Do not let the yolks cook.
- Beat the whites till very stiff but not dry.
- Mix into the chocolate mixture.
- Put in the fridge until set (at least four hours), and serve with cream if you like.

A Wickedly Good Cheesecake

This magnificent pudding has major wow factor and is not nearly as hard as it looks. All the ingredients are easily found and it can be made at any time of year. Keep costs down by using frozen, not fresh, fruit. With the exception of the last step, everything can be prepared ahead

YOU WILL NEED:
A cake tin with a removable base
Parchment paper to line it
A rolling pin
A saucepan
A large mixing bowl
A wooden spoon
A vegetable peeler (for the lemon zest)

INGREDIENTS (FOR 8)
FOR THE BISCUIT-CRUMB BASE
7 digestive biscuits
10 gingernut biscuits
50g unsalted butter

FOR THE FILLING
1 teaspoon of cornflour
4 heaped tablespoons of caster sugar
2 large (300g) tubs of soft cheese
(eg Philadelphia)
a few drops of vanilla essence
zest of one lemon, finely grated
2 eggs
1 large (300ml) tub of soured cream

FOR THE FRUIT TOPPING
400g (large) packet of frozen summer berries or fresh raspberries
3 tablespoons of caster sugar
2 tablespoons of water

- Preheat the oven to 150°C/300°F/gas mark 2.
- Line the base of the cake tin with parchment paper.
- Crush the biscuits into crumbs in a plastic bag by flattening with a rolling pin. Put them in a bowl.
- Melt the butter in a saucepan, pour it over the biscuits and mix, then spoon the mixture into the cake tin. Press the crumbs down with the palm of your hand to form a smooth base. Leave to cool in the fridge.
- In a large bowl mix together the cornflour, sugar, soft cheese, vanilla essence and lemon zest. Then add the eggs and the soured cream and stir again.
- Pour the mixture on top of the crumbs and place in the preheated oven for an hour or a little bit longer until the cake has set. Switch off the oven but leave the cake in for another fifteen minutes. Take it out, allow it to cool, and then chill it in the fridge.
- For the summer fruit topping, dissolve the sugar in a saucepan by adding water and bringing to the boil. Add the summer berries. Cook for a few minutes, then cool.
- Take the cheesecake out of the tin and remove the lining paper, then transfer to a large dish. Strain the berries, spoon over the cake and serve.

Fabulously Gooey Chocolate Brownies

A foolproof recipe for chocolate brownies. Serve warm as a pudding with vanilla ice cream or pack into a rucksack and devour on a beach or mountain.

YOU WILL NEED:
A sharp knife
A small saucepan
A fairly large bowl
An egg whisk (ideally electric)
A sieve
A shallow oven-proof dish
A wooden spoon

INGREDIENTS (FOR 6)
300g (3 standard-sized bars) dark chocolate (eg Lindt 70%), broken into bits
225g (nearly a whole packet) unsalted butter
12 heaped tablespoons of caster sugar
3 eggs
a generous teaspoon of vanilla extract
7 heaped tablespoons of plain flour

- Turn the oven on at 170°C/325°F/gas mark 3 and grease the oven-proof dish.
- Make a few chocolate curls by running a knife along the side of one of the chocolate bars. Next break up the rest of the chocolate into the saucepan and add the butter. Cook over a very low heat until the chocolate has melted and the mixture is smooth. Turn off the heat and allow to cool a little.
- Measure out the sugar and add to the eggs and vanilla extract in the mixing bowl. Lightly whisk the sugar, eggs and vanilla extract together.
- When it is cool enough to dip your finger into it, add the chocolate sauce to the egg and sugar mixture and stir.
- Gradually sift the flour into the mixture, along with a pinch of salt, and fold in gently aiming for a smooth consistency. Taste for sweetness. Pour into the greased dish. Sprinkle the chocolate curls on top.
- Bake for 30 minutes until the top is just set.
- Cut the cooked brownie into squares. Allow to cool before transferring to a plate.

Banana Bread

Everybody adores banana bread and it's particularly scrumptious first thing in the morning with a strong cup of coffee.

YOU WILL NEED:
A wooden spoon
A large bowl
A medium-sized loaf tin
Baking parchment
A vegetable peeler (for the lemon zest)

INGREDIENTS (FOR 1 LOAF)
100g softened butter
2 tablespoons of caster sugar
1 egg
6 tablespoons of plain flour
1 teaspoon of baking powder
4 ripe bananas
a handful of chopped walnuts
2 tablespoons of milk
zest of one lemon

- Heat the oven to 180°C/350°F/gas mark 4. Grease the loaf tin with some butter and line with baking parchment.
- In a large bowl mix together the butter, sugar and egg with a wooden spoon. Then mix in the flour and baking powder. Peel and mash the bananas before adding to the mix. Next add the nuts, the milk and the lemon zest and mix everything together.
- Pour into the loaf tin and bake for an hour.

JUSTIN HARDY

An Easy Apple Cake with Almonds

This delicious cake makes a great dessert or teatime treat and doesn't require a cake tin. It works equally well with plums and nectarines. Serve on individual plates with dollops of crème fraîche.

YOU WILL NEED:
An apple peeler or a sharp knife
A chopping board
A large mixing bowl
A wooden spoon
A medium-sized ovenproof dish

INGREDIENTS (FOR 6)
6 large cooking apples
half a glass of water
ground cinnamon

FOR THE TOPPING
175g unsalted butter (approximately ¾ of a standard packet)
5 heaped tablespoons of caster sugar
2 large free-range eggs
6 heaped tablespoons of self-raising flour
2 tablespoons of ground almonds (sold in some corner shops or in the cake section of supermarkets)

- Preheat the oven to 180°C/350°F/gas mark 4.
- Peel, core and quarter the apples. Cut into thin slices straight into the bottom of the dish. Add the water and sprinkle cinnamon over the apples until nicely covered.
- To make the topping: with a wooden spoon beat together the sugar and butter and eggs in the mixing bowl, sift in the flour and add the ground almonds, and mix thoroughly. Next spread the topping over the apples.
- Bake in the preheated oven for 45 minutes or until golden.

Casilda's Lemon Yoghurt Ice Cream

A lusciously lemony dessert that doesn't require any fancy gadgetry and takes less than five minutes to make. The ice cream is at its best half melted. Decanted onto a big plate and surrounded with chopped strawberries, raspberries or blueberries it makes a stylish and healthy dessert.

YOU WILL NEED:
A bowl
A small plastic container suitable for freezing
A vegetable peeler (for the lemon zest)

INGREDIENTS (FOR 6)
a 500g pot of natural yoghurt
3 lemons (zest of one, plus juice of all three)
4 generous tablespoons of icing sugar
1 small (250ml) pot of double cream

- Place all the ingredients in a bowl and beat together with a fork.
- Decant into a plastic container and seal.
- Freeze for at least 4 hours.

Charles's Cointreau Ice Cream

It's worth schmoozing a tutor, parent or elderly aunt for the small quantity of Cointreau required to make this glamorous ice cream. An electric whisk won't give you arm muscles like Jane Fonda's, but will make the job much easier.

YOU WILL NEED:
A hand or electric whisk
2 largish bowls
A vegetable peeler (for the orange zest)

INGREDIENTS (FOR 8)
4 egg yolks
5 heaped tablespoons of caster sugar
4 tablespoons of Cointreau (or Grand Marnier)
zest of half an orange
a 600ml pot of double cream, whipped

- Add the sugar to the egg yolks and beat like hell until white and fluffy.
- Add the Cointreau and the orange zest. Next add the double cream.
- Put in freezer for 1 hour.
- Remove from freezer, stir and freeze overnight.

Fruits of the Forest Ice Cream

This simple ice cream is a ravishing colour and very easy to make. Thanks to its berry content it also has high levels of antioxidants. Save money by buying the fruit frozen rather than fresh and leave out the cream if you're vegan.

YOU WILL NEED:
A blender
*A small plastic container suitable
for freezing*

INGREDIENTS (FOR 6)
a 500g tub of natural yoghurt
4 heaped tablespoons of icing sugar
*500g packet of frozen forest fruits
(Try the freezer cabinet of your local
Tesco)*
*2 tablespoons of orange liqueur
(optional)*
a small pot of double cream
*almond biscotti (or any biscuits that
take your fancy)*

- Place the yoghurt in a blender with the icing sugar, the frozen forest fruits, the orange liqueur if using and the cream.
- Whizz until blended.
- Spoon into a plastic container, seal and freeze for a few hours.
- Serve semi-melted with almond biscotti, if you like.

JOANNA CHICHESTER-CLARK

Fred's Junket (Milk Pudding)

An old-fashioned, amusingly minimalist recipe that is having a mini-revival (it recently featured on *Masterchef*). This 1985 version can be served with blackberries, raspberries and redcurrants, or try topping it with pistachios, grated nutmeg or cinnamon. It is also good with cream.

YOU WILL NEED:
A saucepan
A wooden spoon
4 tumblers or ramekins for serving

INGREDIENTS (SERVES 4)
1 pint of milk
rennet (sold in large supermarkets)
caster sugar to taste

'First precaution: follow the instructions on the bottle of rennet to discover the ratio of rennet to milk. Heat up milk gently until lukewarm. Add the rennet and stir the milk. Pour the liquid into four small ramekins.

'Second precaution: leave to cool in the open for 20 minutes until set. Then put it in the fridge to chill for about 45 minutes. Never put in fridge straight after heating. Sprinkle sugar over the junket to individual requirements.'

NATACHA LEDWIDGE

STELLA PHIPPS

Yoga While Poaching an Egg

ZEBEDEE HELM

THE STUDENT BREAKFAST & THE COCKTAIL HOUR

Ros's Poached Egg for One

A poached egg followed by a couple of sun salutations is not only the perfect start to the day but a culinary exercise that quickly becomes addictive. When cooked the white should be firm around the runny yolk.

YOU WILL NEED:
A deep-sided frying pan
A small bowl
A clean tea cloth
A toaster
A spoon (ideally slotted)

INGREDIENTS
1 very fresh free-range or organic egg (the fresher the egg, the less likely the white is to float away from the yolk)
a drop of white wine or cider vinegar
a ready-made muffin, sliced in half
unsalted butter

- Take a frying pan and fill one third of it with water. Bring to a gentle simmer.
- Add a drop of white wine or vinegar to the water. (This is meant to prevent the white from breaking away.)
- Put the muffin in the toaster.
- Break the egg into a bowl, then very gently dip the edge of the bowl under the water and launch the egg into the simmering water. If the white spreads out too far, use a spoon to bring it back in.
- Cook the egg for about 3 minutes, basting with the water. Then lift the egg out of the pan with a spoon (trim around the edge if you want it to look neat) and drain on a cloth.
- Serve on the hot buttered muffin.

Edinburgh, November 1985: Ciggies and a full fry-up
Eggs, bacon, toast, fried bread, sausages, cereals, yoghurt,
radio, four newspapers, beer, cigarettes, butter, tea, coffee,
sugar and milk.

Edinburgh, May 2012: The blueberry revolution
Greek or plain yoghurt, granola and blueberries.

The Perfect Dark and Stormy

A Caribbean cocktail that's having a quiet resurgence at London parties.

INGREDIENTS (FOR 1)
2 parts dark Jamaican rum
3 parts ginger beer
dash of lime juice (optional)
ice cubes

- Pour the rum into a tumbler and add the ginger beer, plus lime juice if
  using.
- Allow the fizz to subside. Add the ice cubes.
- Yo-ho-ho!

INKY PAWS PRESS: NATACHA LEDWIDGE

A Stylish Bloody Mary

A classic cocktail that's traditionally served before Sunday lunch. The non-alcoholic version, a Virgin Mary, is exactly the same but without the vodka.

INGREDIENTS (FOR 1)
1 part vodka
3 parts tomato juice
several shakes of Worcestershire sauce
a few drops of Tabasco
a squirt of lemon juice
a sprinkling of celery salt
a slice of lemon to serve
a small stick of celery to serve
(optional)

- Pour the vodka into the bottom of a tumbler or tall glass. Add the tomato juice, followed by the Worcestershire sauce, Tabasco and lemon juice. Sprinkle the celery salt on top.
- Stir with a teaspoon. Decorate with a lemon slice (and celery stick if you like).
- Down the hatch!

A Classic Gin and Tonic

Once associated with elderly men in blazers and striped ties, this fortifying cocktail has been rediscovered by a new generation. G was first added to T in India during the colonial era, as a way of adding pep to quinine (the most effective anti-malaria drug), which is found in tonic water. The Americans did the world a great favour by adding ice. Patrick Dillon, author of a scholarly study of the eighteenth-century gin craze, *The Much-Lamented Death of Madam Geneva*, recommends Plymouth gin, or failing that Tanqueray. The editors rather like Gordon's Export.

INGREDIENTS (FOR 1)
1 part gin
2 to 3 parts tonic water (ideally kept in the fridge)
a slice of lemon
ice cubes

- Pour the gin into a tumbler. Add the tonic – two parts for a strong one, three if you prefer to pace yourself.
- Drop in a slice of lemon and a couple of ice cubes.
- Bottoms up!

Ben's Mississippi Vodka and Watermelon

Watermelon cocktails are madly fashionable and this version made with vodka packs quite a punch. It takes just ten minutes to make, but will need between six and twelve hours of draining time.

YOU WILL NEED:
A sharp knife
A funnel (optional)

INGREDIENTS
1 large (1.5 litre) bottle of vodka
1 large watermelon

'Cut a shallow hole in the melon roughly the size of either the funnel or the vodka bottle top, making sure you pierce only the skin of the melon and not deep into the flesh inside (this can cause dripping during the draining process). The location of the hole is a matter of choice, but many prefer to use either end of the melon in order to allow the melon and bottle to stand alone while draining.

'Remove the cut segment (or plug) and replace with the funnel or up-ended bottle (in the case of the funnel, now fill with vodka). Don't forget to hold onto the plug, as this will be essential in transporting the watermelon (ie to a party). Make sure the melon can stand alone safely, then leave. Remember, this process takes a long time, so do not be disheartened if after an hour the vodka is only a tenth drained.

'An optional step, which can facilitate a more even distribution, is to make multiple holes from which to drain. If this step is taken, be sure to adequately plug existing ones before cutting the new in order to prevent dripping.

'Once all the vodka has drained, eat the watermelon. Be wary – it's not a lot of watermelon, but it is a lot of vodka. This is not a single-serving recipe.

'Optional suggestion: cut the watermelon in half. Use one half for eating, and blend the fruit flesh contents of the other half to make a smoothie. Then use the shell of that half as a punch bowl for said smoothie.'

Elizabeth Peyton-Jones's Hangover Smoothie

Elizabeth is a herbalist and recently wrote a book called *Eat Yourself Young*. This refreshing smoothie is packed with goodness and is made with a healthy dose of cayenne to help you get up and go go. Coconut water comes from the inside of the coconut before you smash it and is different from coconut milk, which is from the pulp. If you can't find coconut water use soya, rice or oat milk instead.

YOU WILL NEED:
A blender

INGREDIENTS (FOR 2)
1 banana
5 or 6 strawberries
a quarter of a cup of blueberries
half a cup of pineapple (supermarkets sell ready-cut chunks near the sandwiches)
one and a half cups of coconut water (available from health food stores or from a fresh coconut)
a dash of cayenne pepper

- Blend all the ingredients together and drink immediately.

Top Student Hangover Remedies

- Philadelphia cheese and Marmite on bagels
- Bacon butties with ketchup
- Tropicana orange juice with bits (especially the bits)
- Diet Coke
- Berocca (supermarket own-brand version)
- Water. Drink lots of it – and wallow
- Paracetamol and/or rehydration salts
- Fish-finger sandwiches

Edwina's Elderflower Syrup

June is the month to make this, when country lanes are awash with frothy bunches of elderflowers. Buy everything you need before collecting the blossoms as they quickly fade after picking (you can freeze the flowers in freezer bags for a year round supply of cordial). Take an umbrella to hook the out-of-reach flowers and wear jeans as protection against nettles. Look for the brightest white flowers and pick them while the sun is shining.

The syrup is like lemonade but with a scented petaly-flowery taste. It can be diluted with still or sparkling water. It's also good poured over vanilla ice-cream.

YOU WILL NEED:
A saucepan
A wooden spoon
A J-cloth or piece of muslin
3 sterilised glass bottles

INGREDIENTS (FOR 3 BOTTLES)
25 heads of elderflowers
1.5kgs caster sugar
4 mugs of water
50g citric acid (you can buy this at a chemist in a 50g box)
1 lemon, chopped

- Pick elderflowers. Encourage any insects to escape.
- Put the sugar in a huge saucepan with the water.
- Leave to boil until all bubbly and the sugar has dissolved. Stir in the citric acid, the elderflowers and the lemon.
- Inhale its scent: delicious!
- Leave overnight. If it does not have the consistency of syrup the next morning, do a little more boiling.
- Strain the liquid through a sieve overlaid with a brand new J-cloth that you have placed in boiling water (or muslin if you have some) into two or three ready-prepared glass bottles that have also been sterilised with boiling water.

Pat's Special Home-made Lemonade

There are few drinks as refreshing as your own lemonade. Buy the best quality lemons you can, avoiding any that are very dark yellow or green. The drink should not taste bitter or cloyingly sweet.

YOU WILL NEED:
A vegetable peeler or paring knife
A chopping board
A lemon squeezer
A large saucepan
A big jug

INGREDIENTS
2 parts lemon juice
1 part caster sugar
3 parts water

- Take a vast number of lemons (about 14 to 16). Zest 8 of them (you will find instructions on zesting on page 95). Make sure there is no white pith or the lemonade will taste bitter.
- Squeeze the juice from all the lemons into a bowl and remove the pips.
- Cover the base of the saucepan with a layer of sugar and add three times as much water. Dissolve the sugar into the water very slowly, not allowing it to boil. Remove the saucepan from the heat.
- Add the lemon zest and lemon juice to the sugar syrup. Leave to cool.
- When it is cold, strain the liquid into a large jug. Add ice cubes and a few slices of lemon. Serve immediately.

Hash Cookies (page 94)

THE NAUGHTY STUFF FROM THE EIGHTIES

KGB officer

KGB tank

ZEBEDEE HELM

Vodka and Bread (overleaf)

The editors take no responsibility for these recipes. We tried to cut them out but they wouldn't go away. Proceed at your own risk!

Vodka and Bread

This dangerously potent cocktail was sent to us in 1985 by a student of Moscow University who had a fight with his room-mate and got thrown out.

'If you don't have too much vodka it is a very simple recipe. The bread must be broken into little pieces and put into the vodka for five minutes. Then eat. I only did this once but the effect was most memorable. It is because the yeast in the bread reacts with the vodka. You can put pepper and salt with it.'

INGREDIENTS (FOR 1)
vodka
bread

Paul's Hash Cookies

• Have a nice day!

MEXICAN TACOS

Chopped Chicken Pieces
(cooked)
Tinned / Creamed Tomatoes
Tomato Puree
Onions (Chopped)
Garlic (optional), cumin, corriander
Salt and Pepper
Red (cooked) Kidney Beans
Taco / Tostada / Tortilla Shells

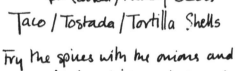

Fry the spices with the onions and
garlic. Add the chicken pieces and continue
to fry for 1 → 2 mins. Add tinned
tomatoes and tomato puree. Cook for
a few more mins. Add kidney beans
shortly before the end.

Serve in Taco Shells
topped with soured
cream and shredded
lettuce.

Best with avocado pear.

THE APOCALYPTIC'S DELIGHT

Inigo's Haricots Noirs à La Merde De Diable

This 1985 dish is extremely adaptable and goes with virtually everything, though it is best with stir-fried cabbage and basmati rice. Not for the faint-hearted.

INGREDIENTS (FOR 5)
5 large handfuls of black beans
1 onion
1 carrot (ideally Spanish though Norwegian is equally suitable)
half a large red pepper
2 teaspoons of asafoetida (Indian spice; essential; quite difficult to get hold of;
crops up in Rabelais; could be imported in sacks)
salt, a sprinkle of pepper to taste
1 teaspoon of ground ginger
2 reasonably hot chillis
enough melted butter to generously cover the bottom of a large frying pan

'Slice the peppers. Chop the onion and slice the carrot. Soaking beans on the whole seems a waste of time, so begin by first boiling them for 15 minutes in a large saucepan. (Unlike red kidney beans, black beans are not likely to give you gastro-enteritis, but this initial stage is worth following for it softens the beans up before you start cooking them properly.) Drain the beans and put them back in the saucepan.

'Fill the saucepan again with enough water so as to completely submerge the beans. Add the onion and carrot. Bring to the boil and simmer for an hour to an hour and a half. Melt the butter in a large frying pan and when about to burn, add the sliced red pepper. Cook for 4 minutes on a high flame.

'Sprinkle asafoetida into the pan. When this starts to burn (normally after 30 seconds) start to spoon the beans and the liquid into the pan. At this point either flambé the beans (which is not hard to do because if you have a gas stove the butter will invariably catch alight) or, the more cautious approach, turn off the gas, and then add the beans and liquid. Add the rest of the ingredients and cook on a medium heat until the liquid has thickened (approx 15 minutes). Eat immediately.'

NATACHA LEDWIDGE

KITCHEN SAVVY

Safety measures

- Keep raw and cooked food separate, and never prepare them using the same knife or chopping board without washing it scrupulously in between
- Raw meat should be kept in a shallow dish at the bottom of the fridge where it can't drip onto other foods
- Do not put hot food in the fridge as it will warm up the air inside and encourage the growth of bacteria
- Throw out any food that's worrying you. Three days is quite long enough for most cooked food to live in the fridge
- Wrap up butter or cream as they absorb flavours from other foodstuffs
- Never leave a sharp knife in the sink or pointing upwards in a dishwasher where it will be a hazard for the unwary
- When reheating food always make sure it is piping hot in order to kill off any bacteria
- Chicken or pork must always be cooked through. If the meat is pink or the juices run pink rather than clear, put them back in the oven.

Tricks of the trade

How to Chop Vegetables

To dice an onion Peel and cut in half through the root end. Place the halves cut side down and cut thin vertical slices up to but not through the root end. Holding the knife flat, cut thin horizontal slices up to but not through the root end. Finally, cut the onion crosswise so that it falls into chopped pieces.

To deseed and chop a chilli Halve the chilli lengthways and scrape out the seeds and core with a knife. Slice the flesh into half-rings. After cutting chillis always wash your hands thoroughly with soap, as chillis contain capsaicin, which is an irritant. Whatever you do, don't rub your eyes.

To deseed large peppers Slice off the stem end and scrape out the seeds.

To zest a lemon First wash the lemon, then peel the skin off using a vegetable peeler, avoiding any bitter white pith. Place the bits of peel on a flat surface and chop into little strips.

How to make stock

Chicken stock Rather than waste a leftover chicken carcass, put it in a large saucepan and cover with water. Add an onion (peeled and quartered), a carrot (peeled and quartered), a celery stalk if you have one, and one or two herbs such as parsley and thyme. Bring to the boil and simmer for an hour. Strain and let cool. You can use it the next day for soup (it will keep for two days in the fridge) or freeze it in ice trays for another time. To use, melt the cubes and dilute with water to taste.

Vegetable stock Vegetables are the only thing that *nobody* steals from the fridge, and often end up languishing there for too long. Boil any onions, carrots, leeks, celery stalks and courgettes that are beginning to look tired in a saucepan with parsley, thyme and peppercorns. Simmer for 30 minutes. Strain. Use the vegetable stock for soup or freeze, as above.

When supplies are really low

Cheap Edible Leftovers (1985)

Bubble and squeak (Cathy Milner, Edinburgh College of Art).
Mix leftover vegetables with mashed potatoes and fry them all up.

Polish ancestral slosh (Tim Makower, Architecture, Cambridge).
Pork mince, boiled cabbage, chopped onions and garlic and lots of wine. All fried.

Russian rations (Russian student, Edinburgh).
Fried onions, potatoes and garlic.

NATACHA LEDWIDGE

Kettle cooking

It is possible (but not recommended) to cook boiled eggs, pasta and frankfurters in your kettle. One technique is to use the sort of netting that onions come bagged in to put the food in the kettle and take it out again. However, do not try cooking pasta sauce as it will ruin the electrics (see 'Pastaargh: pasta, cooked with a kettle' on YouTube). And heating up a can of soup in the electric kettle will make all the posters peel off your walls.

Oeuf à la kettle

YOU WILL NEED:
A kettle
Supermarket netting

INGREDIENTS (FOR 1)
1 medium-sized egg

- Fill kettle with water and boil.
- Place the egg in the netting and carefully lower into kettle until completely submerged. Put the kettle lid on, but with the netting over the edge.
- Keep turning the kettle on again to keep the water boiling.
- Leave for 3 minutes until cooked.
- Do not leave for too long or the egg will explode.

Gruesome trivia

Don't Try To Live Off Porridge
The last known case of scurvy in the British Isles was a veterinary student at Edinburgh who lived entirely off porridge, pre-cooked in huge quantities, until he was taken into hospital.

Beware of the Burger
Oxford High Street was for many years the favourite parking spot of a mobile caterer whose best-selling product was known to students as the Death Burger.

On the Dangers of Overeating
'The death of great men is not always of proportion to the lustre of their lives. The death of Pope was imputed by some of his friends to a silver saucepan, in which it was his delight to heat potted lampreys,' wrote Dr Johnson in his *Lives of the Poets*. King Henry 1 is also reported to have died of a surfeit of lampreys, and King John of a surfeit of peaches.

EDINBURGH DIGEST

In Which the Author, Crispin Jackson, Makes a Sentimental Journey through the Eateries and Carry-Outs of the Old University City

A CENTURY AGO, so grey heads tell us, it was considered bad form to discuss food; now, the British talk about little else, which might cause some to question the appearance of yet another cookbook.

But as well as the simple fact that the recipes contained herein are varied, original and easy to prepare, this book has one further distinction: its sheer unlikeliness. For no group has better reason for neglecting the kitchen than students, who have so many other places to go for food.

Indeed, looking back on my own undergraduate years in Edinburgh, I recall very little learning, but a great deal of eating, most of it done away from home, in the many cafes and canteens within, or adjoining, the campus. The various university eateries could be graded as for a Michelin guide: one star was a pie in one of the union bars; two stars, haggis and neeps in the nearest refectory. Three stars was some sort of roast in the restaurant opposite McEwan Hall, where students ate beneath the plaster gaze of Edinburgh's most famous alumnus, Thomas Carlyle, and were served by a team of bloused and ancient ladies who might have been Caledonian cousins to the old dear who kept the buffet counter in *Brief Encounter*.

Next door was a private dining room, which was the nearest Edinburgh came to the top table of Oxbridge colleges. On one occasion here, I listened to a former Conservative Prime Minister bemoaning the failings of the British electorate (something to do with a national obsession with beefeaters and their like), while enjoying the best roast beef, and the best claret, I have ever tasted. If that was my sole experience of formal dining during my time at Edinburgh, I am quite happy.

Restaurants were plentiful in Edinburgh, especially Italian ones (very proud of their Italian settlers, are the Scots), but most of the city's eating is done outside, on its cold and cobbled streets. For, as well as being the loveliest city

in the British Islands, and having the biggest arts festival – and the finest small art gallery – in Europe, Edinburgh has at least one further distinction: it is the world capital of 'carry-outs'. Indeed, by far the most famous eatery in the whole city is the Alba D'Oro Fish and Chip Shop on Henderson Row at the bottom of Georgian New Town, its walls garnished with stuffed and varnished game fish, its fryers teeming with an astonishing range of processed fish and flesh.

Better still were the city's many bakeries which, with an obligingness one doesn't normally associate with British businesses, sold their products at the back door during the small hours when the actual baking was done. Few experiences can compare with the rapture of a student drunk staggering home at three in the morning with a bag of oven-hot doughnuts, steak pasties and mince pies: not the yuletide variety, but the Scottish speciality of peppered mutton stew enclosed in a cup of pastry so short it resembles the turn-downs on a fisherman's boots.

'THIS IS, ABOVE ALL, A GOOD-NATURED, EVEN JOYOUS BOOK, ALIVE WITH THE EXCITEMENT OF EXPERIMENTATION AND DISCOVERY'

Other university cities have their gastronomic glories: Manchester its multi-storey Chinese restaurants, Leicester and Birmingham their numerous curry houses. Oxford has dear old Browns, and what used to be an excellent buffet at the Randolph Hotel, served in a room full of Osbert Lancaster oils. It's a wonder that any student stays in to cook at all.

(Continued overleaf)

INKY PAWS PRESS

(Continued from previous page)

The recipes in *Goodbye Cockroach Pie* are eclectic and imaginative in their merging of ingredients and national cuisines. They are mercifully free of such Beetonesque imprecations as 'Prepare a white sauce', or autobiographical ramblings of the sort that make Elizabeth David's books so intimidating for the novice chef.

Of course, all can be tailored to individual tastes; I do not think that any of their creators would mind. For this is, above all, a good-natured, even joyous book, alive with the excitement of experimentation and discovery.

'BETTER STILL WERE THE CITY'S MANY BAKERIES WHICH SOLD THEIR PRODUCTS AT THE BACK DOOR DURING THE SMALL HOURS'

Revisiting old haunts can be a painful business, as I discovered when, on a rare return visit to Edinburgh, I sought out a once-favourite café in a little street that curled down from the Old College to the much more ancient Old Town. My delight that the menu was unchanged – thin soup, steak pie with suet pastry, jam roll and custard – was shattered when the the pinny-ed waitress proudly announced that the place would soon be going upmarket, like so much of Edinburgh: 'We'll be doing Italian food, something a bit more upper-class.' But if cooks and kitchens are all too ephemeral, cooking is enduring, though ever-changing.

In a food-obsessed world, these dishes will revive your appetite, not just for eating, but for the simple pleasure of cooking for – and sharing a table with – friends old and new.

POTS, PANS & ESSENTIAL KIT

JOANNA CHICHESTER-CLARK

Most people arrive at university with a few pots and pans. Here is our beginner's guide to handy kitchen equipment.

On the shelf

Not having enough **mugs** can cause a major break-down in harmonious communal living. Cheap **wine glasses** if you are a keen wine drinker (breakages are common so don't waste your money on posh ones). A **cafetière** for serious coffee drinkers and a **coffee grinder** for extra-serious ones (you can also use it for grinding spices; otherwise you will need a **pestle and mortar**).

In the drawer

You can never have too many **wooden spoons** or too much **cutlery**.

(Continued overleaf)

Other essentials

A **tin opener**.

A **corkscrew** (the **Screwpull** ones are reliable and easy to use).

A **sharp all-purpose knife** (a 15cm/6inch one is a good size). It should have a secure grip and feel comfortable in your hand. Also a serrated **bread knife** and ideally a small **paring knife**.

A **fish slice** or **spatula** for turning meat or fish when frying; also essential for omelettes.

A **vegetable peeler** – all-important for peeling spuds.

A **box grater** or the very sharp, more modern **Microplane grater** with a handle (used by professional chefs).

Cling film; **tin foil**; clean **tea towels**; **bin liners**.

Dark glasses (any old ones) for chopping onions.

Behind the sink

A **large plastic chopping board**. **Washing-up liquid**, a **scrubbing brush** and other cleaning equipment.

By the stove

Absolutely essential: a **medium-sized heavy-based saucepan** that conducts the heat evenly, and a **non-stick frying pan**.

A **wok**: essential for speedy stir-frying, it brings cheffy drama to the kitchen. There are several types but a 35cm/14inch carbon-steel flat-bottomed one is generally recommended. The main thing is it has to be heavy to distribute the heat so the food won't burn. To see a master at work (with 12 woks on the go) look up 'King of Wok' on YouTube.

It is also useful to have a **casserole dish** that can go either on top of the hob or inside the oven, and a **roasting tin**. A **heavy cast iron griddle**, although quite specialised and expensive, produces healthy smoky-flavoured food without any of the hassle of a barbecue. And don't forget **oven gloves**.

In the cupboard

A **sieve** and a **colander**.
A **lemon squeezer**.
A **non-stick baking tray**.
A **non-stick 20cm/8inch cake tin**
(the ones with separate bases are easy
to use). At a pinch you can use the
cake tin as a flan dish, which is also
nice to have. A **loaf tin** for any kind
of bread-making.
Some small **storage boxes** or
Tupperware for leftovers.

On the kitchen table

Tea candles – you can buy these
cheaply in bulk and they will cheer
up any scene. A **measuring jug** that
doubles up as a vase or a milk jug.

Electricals

One of the great mysteries of modern
life is how often electrical equipment
breaks down. If you are sharing the
kitchen with other students it is a
good idea to club together to buy a
toaster and a **kettle** – though more
often than not everyone brings one
and you end up with 10 of each.
A **blender** or **liquidiser**: either hand-
held or in a jug shape. Especially
good for vegans, vegetarians and
anyone fond of home-made dips,
salsas, smoothies and soups.
An **electric whisk**: essential for
whisking egg whites for chocolate
mousse and cakes.
A **juicer**: definitely not cheap, but
home-made fruit and vegetable juices
give an instant health boost.
A **microwave**: this is very handy
for a small kitchen and useful for
defrosting discounted meat or fish. It
is worth checking the power setting
as this can vary (from 800w to 1000w
for example). The cooking times for
shop-bought microwave meals are
usually set for 800w.

Lastly

Kitchen scales – no kitchen scales
are necessary for *Goodbye Cockroach
Pie* but once you have them you will
be able to follow the recipes in any
cookbook confidently and feel like
a 'watcher of the skies/When a new
planet swims into his ken' (Keats,
*On First Looking into Chapman's
Homer*: discuss with reference to (a)
Romanticism and (b) advances in
nineteenth-century astronomy).

INDEX

Rosanna Kelly's books include *Russia* and *The Little Book of Wit and Wisdom*

Casilda Grigg (left) is the former food and drink editor of the *Daily Telegraph*